D1323914

Happy Writing

Reviews

I love this book! Beautifully written, it's full of practical, down to earth advice, as well as more thought-provoking passages, and things I'd never thought of, or didn't know, before.

Abi Burlingham, author and artist

An invaluable addition to your writer's bookshelf. I have recommended it to several authors and will be rereading it myself as I need to.

Cressida Dowling, The Book Analyst

Inspiring, enabling, but not at all wishy washy – it rightly emphasizes the necessity of working at this craft.

Gill Payne, aspiring writer

Most writing manuals are aimed at people seeking publication for the first time, whereas Alexander has much to say about mid- or late-career crises in which a writer can feel stale, even trapped by success, and in need of a fresh approach.

Linda Newbery, Costa Book Prize

Jenny writes in such an easy, friendly and re-assuring style that it's tempting, if you are a galumphing reader like me, to speed through the pages. I'd advise reading this book with a pencil in hand, underlining sentences that resonate, and suggestions that require deeper pondering...

Penny Dolan, children's author

A philosophy which will make you feel even better about your writing life.

Alex Gutteridge, children's author

HAPPY WRITING

BEAT YOUR BLOCKS, BE PUBLISHED AND FIND YOUR FLOW

JENNY ALEXANDER

five
lanes

A non-writing writer is a monster courting insanity.
Franz Kafka

Published by Five Lanes Press, 2017.

Contact info@fivelanespress.co.uk

Previously published in 2015 as *When a Writer Isn't Writing: How to Beat Your Blocks, Be Published and Find Your Flow.*

Contact author@jennyalexander.co.uk

Website www.jennyalexander.co.uk

ISBN: 978-1-910300-14-5 (Paperback)

978-1-910300-15-2 (eBook)

Cover design by Rachel Lawson http://www.lawstondesign.com

Design and typesetting: Zebedee Design

Contents

Introduction

Recently, I noticed I was feeling a bit gloomy. Nothing epic, just a kind of flatness and a sense that life was somehow passing me by. I could have looked for psychological explanations for my low mood but when I noticed how I was feeling I knew immediately what was causing it – I wasn't writing.

I was working flat-out on my writing career, organising my workshop programme for the year ahead, updating my blog and self-publishing my child-of-the-heart book, *Writing in the House of Dreams*, but what that came down to was day after day of looking at diaries, sending enquiries, penning publicity, seeking permissions, researching services, making decisions... and not writing.

I had half a dozen ideas for new books waiting to be written, including this book about writing. Someone in the industry had put me off by saying the market was already saturated with books by writers about writing and I'd never find a publisher but now, with the possibility of self-publishing, it had gone to the top of my list.

I have always been a very happy writer – in the professional groups I belong to, it's kind of my Unique Selling Point. In a wonderful, varied writing career, creative satisfaction has been my priority and my goal, so I've really focused on learning how to deal with anything that gets in the way of that. The book I wanted to write was for all the writers I knew who struggled with blocks and problems, which I had found all kinds of ways of tackling.

So there I was, gloomily surveying my to-do lists and realising the reason I was feeling fed up was because I wasn't writing, when three things happened that gave me the nudge I needed.

First, a friend in the Scattered Authors Society posted a message to the group about not being able to write, and feeling completely bereft. A slew of sympathetic messages came in from dozens of other authors who knew the feeling and made great suggestions including that she should go for walks, do a different kind of creative work for a while and... read books about writing.

I've got a whole shelf of books about writing and some of them have become old friends. I thought, of course writers write about writing and of course they read about it, and given the explosion of opportunities for writers, it would take a complete deluge of books about writing to saturate the market.

The second thing that happened was that someone at one of my workshops asked me if I was the Jenny Alexander who had written the children's book, *How to be a Brilliant Writer*, that she had seen in Maeve Binchy's recommended reading at the back of *The Maeve Binchy Writers' Club*, so I felt I really did have something to say for adult writers too.

The third thing was that I happened upon a blog post about making time even in the busiest schedule for regular writing; you don't just find it, the blogger said, you have to create it.

So I decided to set aside every morning for writing this

book, and push the non-writing side of being an author back to the afternoons. As soon as I made that decision, it was like the sun bursting through from behind the clouds, because when this writer is writing, all is right with the world.

I'm going to love writing this book; I hope you will love reading it too. I'm writing it for every writer who isn't writing – which from time to time is all of us.

1 When You Can't Get Started

So you've got a great idea for a book, and the more you think about it the more excited you feel. It's going to be amazing. It's going to be perfect!

If the idea stays with you, it becomes more and more intriguing; it takes over your mind like the madness of falling in love. You think about it all the time, you dream about it, you stop in the middle of brushing your teeth or buying your groceries to jot down some notes.

As infatuation turns towards commitment, you go into a new phase, planning and organising, working out the detail, creating as much of an outline as you personally need in order to start writing, until the day finally comes when you're ready to begin.

You tidy your desk and clear your calendar. You open a new document, look at the screen. Check Facebook, just quickly. See what's happening in Twitter. You go back to your new document and write the title. Check Facebook again, make some coffee, come back and look at your screen.

You write a few lines, delete them, write a few more. Eat things. Look at your screen. You think about all the jobs you should be doing, such as renewing your car insurance or getting someone in to mend the garden shed.

You seek out distractions, and then resent them for taking you away from your writing. The more you put off starting, the stronger your desire grows, and the deeper your frustration.

It makes no sense. You know what you want to write – so why can't you just take the plunge?

Impatience is a form of resistance

If you've got a great idea but can't get started, you may simply be trying to start too soon. In our target-driven culture, we tend to try and short-cut the first stage of the creative process because doodling and daydreaming, walking, observing, moving objects around in your mind can seem like wasting time.

Actually, it is the heart and depth of everything, the place that writing springs from, and the fact that it's pleasurable probably also contributes to the feeling that it isn't really work.

At this early stage you may not be getting words on the page, but you are laying vital groundwork without which, if you try to start writing the book prematurely, you may end up making false starts or not getting started at all.

Sometimes, if you can't get started, you just need to go back and spend a little more time pondering and playing. In the long run, this is always time well spent, because when you hold off from starting before your idea is really ready, the writing tends to run more smoothly and be finished more quickly.

I often have a great idea but can't seem to get started. It's usually because I haven't given myself space and time to get to know my characters well enough. So I need to keep thinking about them in my head and usually one will start taking over and needing to be heard.

Nicola Morgan

The period of preparation may take a few minutes or a few weeks; every book is different. It may take months or even years, with breaks away from it in between.

A first book, for example, can feel like a spontaneous eruption, because characters, stories and ideas that have been building up in the author's psyche for years are suddenly released. Many authors expect the next book to be ready just as quickly, and then suffer second book syndrome.

If you've done plenty of pondering for the book you want to write and know your characters really well, another possibility as to why you can't get started is that you might not have enough of a plan. Every writer has different criteria when it comes to planning, so this isn't necessarily about knowing all the details, just about knowing enough for you.

For myself, when I'm writing non-fiction, I need an idea of the scope and structure of the book and the main areas I'm going to be exploring, but I don't need a detailed plan of anything except the first few chapters; I prefer to work it out as I go along.

My approach is similar when I'm writing fiction; I need a plan of the first few chapters, a strong idea of the ending, to give me a sense of direction, and a sketchy bit in the middle where I don't really know what's going to happen.

That sketchy bit is very important for me. On

occasions when I've been asked for a full chapter-by-chapter outline before I've written the book, I've found that it takes all the pleasure out of the actual writing. It turns the first draft into a join-the-dots exercise rather than a delicious voyage of discovery, and I can't get excited about it.

Some writers just need a sense of what their protagonist wants, and they're off on a wing and a prayer. Others aren't ready to start writing until they have a filing cabinet full of notes and a detailed plot description.

> It's often assumed that a good plot idea is enough to get a story started – but that's only the jumping-off point. I never feel ready to begin a novel until I've decided on the structure, and maybe experimented a bit. That means: whose story is it? Will I have one viewpoint, two, or several? Will the telling be in the first-person or third? Present tense or past? Will the story be told chronologically, or will it move back and forth in time? The answers to these questions determine so much about the novel's perspectives.
>
> Linda Newbery

If you feel that you've done all the preparation and planning you need but still can't get started, it might be simply a question of getting in the zone. Whether it's your first book or your fifty-first, whether you're struggling to write the opening pages or the beginning of individual chapters and paragraphs, a degree of delay and frustration can be a normal part of the creative process.

I often have to spend several days wrestling with my

thoughts and ideas, trying to find the right words and repeatedly failing, before suddenly the clouds lift and I can see how to begin.

It's the same when you're trying to make a choice or decision in your daily life, gathering information, weighing up pros and cons until you can't see the wood for the trees, and just when you feel like giving up, you wake up one morning knowing what you need to do.

Your unconscious, dreaming mind will take over and make sense of your mental muddle, but it only kicks in when you're actively and intensively focusing your day mind on the problem in hand.

So all that seemingly fruitless effort and concentration when you're trying to write but not getting anywhere is actually serving a purpose and the quickest, most efficient way of dealing with it is simply to accept it, even though it feels so challenging.

Delay and frustration are part of the creative process and, if you want to be a happy writer, you have to learn to bear it. The key is patience, which the Oxford English Dictionary defines as 'the capacity to accept or tolerate delay, problems, or suffering without becoming annoyed or anxious'.

At this stage in my own process I think of the Zen teaching, 'great faith, great doubt, great effort'.

In order not to feel annoyed or anxious, you need to have faith that during times when you're pushing and pushing but can't seem to make any headway, something is happening at a deep level, and your unconscious mind is finding the way.

You need to have doubt in the sense that, although you've got a plan, you are still open to new possibilities and willing to let your instinct, or unconscious mind, guide you.

Finally, you need to try, try and go on trying, puzzling over your plot and worrying at your words, until the way becomes clear.

You can enable this process by faith, doubt and effort, but you can't force the pace. The unconscious mind takes as long as it takes. When I was first starting out, I bombarded my new agent with manuscripts which were half-baked and nowhere near publishable quality.

The more she rejected, the more I sent, until she told me to calm down, stop trying to rush things and take my time. I felt indignant, until I chanced upon a sentence in something I was reading, which helped me understand: 'Impatience is a form of resistance.'

I copied it out and stuck it on the wall above my desk. It reminds me that sometimes writing doesn't go the way we want it to, or the way we feel it should, especially when we're putting in the hard yards but not seeming to get anywhere.

Effort and willpower are important but they're not enough on their own. They are our invitation to the muse who, frustrating as it may be, will not be rushed; she will come in her own sweet time.

Could fear be holding you back?

Impatience can be a problem in the writing process, whether it's trying to start before you've done enough preparation and planning, or expecting the writing to flow as soon as you sit down to write.

But sometimes not being able to start isn't so much about a problem in the process as a hidden resistance in the writer's self. Whenever you feel stuck, it might be worth asking yourself whether fear could be holding you back.

I'm guessing you're wondering now whether to give this section a miss – I mean, what's to be afraid of? Writing isn't exactly an extreme sport.

But whenever something you want to happen doesn't happen, even though it's within your capabilities, nine times out of ten, fear is at the bottom of it. None of us likes to admit we're feeling afraid, even to ourselves, so rather than acknowledging it we usually try to explain it away.

The most common reason people give for not writing when they really want to is that they haven't got time. This might be true but then again, what about all those bestselling authors who wrote their first books in the small hours of the morning when the rest of the world was asleep, or in lunch and coffee breaks, or vacations at home in front of the computer instead of sitting on a sunny beach?

William Carlos Williams wrote his poems on the back of his prescription pad between patients; Philip Larkin produced poems and novels whilst working for thirty years as a university librarian. I personally know lots of successful children's authors who manage to fit their writing in around family commitments or demanding jobs such as teaching.

If you feel the reason you're stuck is because you haven't got time for writing, put that idea under the microscope. Have you really got no time at all, or could that apparent reason be masking some deeper fear?

Take this book, for example. Until a few weeks ago, I thought the reason I hadn't started writing it was because

I simply didn't have time, what with all the demands of self-publishing my dream book and organising my workshops.

But when the conversation about writer's block came up in the Scattered Authors' chat-room, and then someone told me Maeve Binchy had recommended my children's book on writing, and then I read the blog about creating time for writing rather than waiting for it to appear, suddenly I was able to start, even though nothing external had changed.

I still had a long to-do list; I still felt as if it would take me months to clear it. The fact that I was able to start my book anyway shows that the real problem wasn't lack of time – it was the fear planted by the person who told me the market was saturated with writers' books on writing and I would be wasting my time.

I was afraid that after all the work of writing the book, nobody would want to read it, and that is a perfectly reasonable fear. Here are some other common fears that might hold you back when you're thinking about beginning a new book.

Fear of commitment

Writing a book is a huge undertaking. It takes a long time and a lot of hard work. It means long periods of being on your own, neglecting your family and friends and missing out on other things you'd like to do.

It can take over your life to an extraordinary extent, occupying your mind around the clock and making it hard to achieve any kind of work-life balance. It can disturb your sleep and keep you awake at night.

Writing can also unsettle you because, once started, it can develop its own momentum and take its own pathways into areas of your psyche you didn't know about and don't want to explore.

The writing might flow for 50,000 words, only to suddenly run out of steam, or you might get right to the end, no problem, but realise it's rubbish when you come to read back through it.

Your book might not find a publisher, or it might find one but then go quickly out of print. Your publisher might put no effort into promoting it but keep it in print despite very low sales, so that you can't reclaim the rights and try a different route to market.

The fact is, there's no way of knowing, when you start writing, how it will progress; there's no guarantee of a good creative outcome, or of earning any income from all your hard work. You would be mad not to feel some reluctance to commit.

Fear of failure

Fear of failure is part of the quality-control process. You have to consider the possibility of failure in order to weigh up whether your book has a reasonable chance of achieving some kind of success, either as a satisfying creative experience for you, a joy for readers, a bread-and-butter earner or a massive money-spinner. How you measure success will depend upon your personal goals and motivations.

This fear of failure carries right through the whole process, from starting writing to redrafting, pitching and publication, because there's a real possibility of failure at every point along the way and, unlike most areas of life, putting in a massive amount of effort may not increase your chances of avoiding it. In writing, effort is not related to rewards.

Fear of feeling exposed

Another common fear can be around feeling exposed. In everything you write, you inevitably reveal part of yourself, and when your book is published, anyone can read you, judge you and have an opinion about you.

The same feeling can kick in at any stage in your career, whenever you produce a book that's different from what you've written before, and so reveals you in a different way.

Fear of responsibility

A fear I know has held me back at times in my own writing has been the fear of responsibility. A book is a powerful thing. When you write, you plant images and ideas in other people's minds, which can have a positive or negative impact on their lives.

Thirty years ago, I read a murder mystery which included a completely unexpected and very graphic scene of violence which I have never managed to forget; it comes back to me every time I use a common household product. I'm glad I didn't create that scene and put it in someone else's mind. Other books have included passages that have inspired and guided me ever since, and I would be proud to have written them.

You have to take responsibility for the effects your

writing may have on other people. If you are writing fiction you are creating experiences for your readers; if memoir or autobiography, you are telling a story that isn't only yours to tell, and will affect how others see those closest to you.

If you are writing biography, you are making a real person's life into fiction because the selection of material and the literary devices you employ to make it readable will inevitably distort and interpret the facts, yet you are presenting it as a factual account.

If you are writing non-fiction, you have to be sure you know what you're talking about because people give books a special kind of authority.

When I was thinking about writing self-help books for children, especially on the subject of bullying, I was worried about giving advice in case any of my young readers misunderstood what I was suggesting or tried to do what I suggested and it didn't work.

I came up against the same block more recently when I was thinking about writing a book on dreams. Most people are happy to more-or-less ignore their dreams and it might be argued that ignorance is bliss. Dreams will take you to very dark places, as well as very wonderful ones. They may bring startling clarity to your understanding of waking life, but also deep confusion.

Dreams are complicated. Becoming more aware of them is a road to new experience and understanding, but it is not necessarily a road to happiness. To cross that border and take the exploration ever deeper might not be a positive and life enhancing experience for every reader, and could be quite unsettling.

Fear of criticism and rejection

Criticism hurts. Criticism of something you've put your heart and soul into for months or years of your life can feel almost unbearable, and I've met lots of talented people who have given up on writing after their first readers' feedbacks or publishers' rejections.

At least most publishers are polite and positive, and reviewers in the mainstream media usually try to be fair. These days though, as soon as you put a book out anybody can publicly slate it, even if they haven't read it.

I've got a reader review in amazon.com at the moment for *Bullies, Bigmouths and So-called Friends* which states that the book recommends children hitting back; it most certainly does not, but there's nothing I can do to get it taken down (I've tried).

A review of *Writing in the House of Dreams* on the same site questions my sanity and says I'm boring.

The point is, when you publish in this digital age you put yourself and your tender young book in the firing line and there are people out there who will delight in shooting you down.

Fear of success

I think fear of success is the mother of all fears because if you become successful the stakes are raised. The fear of failure could kick in even more strongly when you've had one best-selling book, because the pressure will be on you to write another, and what if you can't?

If your book is a bestseller, the media will take more

interest in you and that can be hard to handle and control, so the fear of feeling exposed could kick in big time.

The higher your profile, the more people will read you and take you seriously, which could exacerbate any fear you have of responsibility.

Success breeds jealousy and resentment, so the higher your profile the more you might attract the attention of people who want to bring you down with critical feedback and reviews.

As well as exacerbating other anxieties, success could bring consequences you might not want. Supposing your YA novel about self-harming sells, your publisher will certainly want more in the same vein, and that could commit you to a long period immersed in teenage angst, when you might prefer to take a break and work on something light and funny.

Supposing you become a very successful children's author but you want to write raunchy romances as well, your publisher will not be happy about you risking damage to your wholesome children's author persona by pursuing this new direction.

Increasingly in the modern market, success means building a brand. It means producing books of the same kind at an industrial pace, leaving little time for other creative ventures. One of the joys of obscurity is that you're free to explore all the highways and byways of your own creativity.

Finally, if you like your life the way it is, success will certainly change things, and you might be afraid of losing what you've got.

Of course, fear isn't always a bad thing. The function of

fear is to keep you safe. For example, the fear of committing to a new book may protect you from starting something at the wrong time, which will only give you stress. Life can't always accommodate the high demands of writing.

When I started my career I had two children in school and two in playgroup and I was worried because all I'd written previously was adult fiction in my teens and twenties, and I knew how completely absorbing and compulsive that could become.

I loved being a stay-at-home mother, so I decided the way for me to be a writer and still feel happily focused on family life was if I stuck to writing for children. Writing children's stories sweeps you up in the same way as writing for adults, but it comes in much shorter bursts.

While the world of your adult novel may call you in and carry you away for upwards of a year, a short children's story may take only weeks or months, and each scene or chapter is much shorter.

I did write for adults when my children were little, but I stuck to non-fiction, because that doesn't take you into another world like fiction; it anchors you very much in this one, and you can break it down into manageable pieces and focus on one topic or area at a time, so it's much easier to pick up and put down.

These days, I'm wary of starting a new project unless I can block in a couple of months on the calendar without any house guests or trips away; even the possibility of major distractions can make me hold back.

There have been periods (my husband's last illness e.g.), when I haven't even tried to write. I also took a year off when we moved house from Manchester to Cambridge in 2010.

Adèle Geras

When you are ready to start writing, fear of commitment may help you to make appropriate choices about what to write and when to write it.

Supposing the book you want to write is a thinly veiled account of wife-swapping in your street, and you're anxious about the effect it might have on your relationship with your neighbours, that fear of responsibility might be flagging up a real danger and making you think it through thoroughly before you start.

But although fear can be the voice of common sense, most often it's the voice of habit so deeply ingrained that you're scarcely aware of it. The particular things you're afraid of are part of your personality: their original function was to keep you safe, but their actual effect may be to keep you small.

I kept myself out of my writing, never stood for anything and never let my writing become personal. Looking back now, I understand that I was terrified of failing and making mistakes. Being invisible kept me safe from criticism and rejection.

The decision to remain invisible kept me protected for years, until it didn't any more. My mind had to invent new ways of keeping me small. This often led to self-sabotage and eventually writer's block.

The day I made the decision to become visible and shine is the day I changed my life as a writer. I decided to show myself in writing, to share all my failures, my successes with readers.

Vangile Makwakwa

Fear can get in the way of your writing at any stage, but fortunately there are simple strategies based on cognitive behavioural therapy that you can use to handle it.

How to handle fear

Sometimes you will be well aware that fear is holding you back, as I was when I put off writing my children's self-help books and adult book on dreams, fearing the responsibility of sharing ideas and suggestions that readers might find unhelpful or confusing.

But fear can also work on a completely unconscious level. Like anger, it feels bad; it may offend our self-image or present a challenge we don't want to recognise, so we commonly deflect, disguise and deny it.

Therefore, the first step when it comes to handling fear is to simply become aware of it, to root it out and identify what you might be afraid of.

First... identify your fears

A simple way to spot when fear is holding you back is by listening to your 'self-talk'. It might surprise you, once you start to notice, what kinds of thing you tell yourself all the time, without even realising you're doing it.

If you catch yourself thinking:

- 'I'm not good enough... My idea isn't good enough... I won't be able to finish it... It'll never get published...' then fear of failure might be holding you back.
- 'No one will like it... It'll make me look pompous/ flippant/boring/ill-informed...' fear of going public and being exposed to criticism is in the mix.
- 'Readers might not understand what I mean... they might be upset by it... the ideas that work for me might not work for them...' this kind of self-talk could flag up fear of responsibility.
- 'My friends might be jealous... I might have to appear at festivals... I might be sent on book tours all over the world...' may mean you have a fear of success unless, of course, those thoughts fill you with joy.

Simply noticing your self-talk makes a difference because you become aware that there's more to your block than the rational explanations your fears might be hiding behind. When you can see the real problem, you can deal with it.

Next... press pause

The way we react to fear, like fear itself, often works on an unconscious level. We go into automatic responses of fight, flight or freeze, which are instinctive and irrational.

The next stage in handling fear the cognitive way, having brought your fear to the surface where you can see it, is to notice your automatic response and press pause. Going straight into fight, flight or freeze can cause all manner of disruption in your writing life.

Take the fear of failure, for example, which is commonly triggered by rejection. If publishers turned down something I'd written I used to go straight into fear – 'What's the point? I can't do this. I'll never be able to do this' – and that mindset was like a swamp that sucked me down and paralysed my writing for weeks or even months at a time. That's freeze.

I've met authors whose response to rejection, and the fear of failure it provokes, has been to fight. 'My book is as good as Harry Potter! Publishers just aren't getting it. I'm going to make them eat their words!'

These authors will put all their energy into pushing, promoting and arguing over the rejected piece and leave themselves no time for working on new projects. That's fight. It might be active but it's just as damaging to the creative flow as the inertia of those who naturally freeze.

Rejection doesn't have to be a complete closing of the door. Just because a book isn't publishable right now and in its present form does not mean there's nothing in it that might be of publishable quality in some form and at some future time.

But I've met writers who have abandoned a project completely and for ever because it has been turned down. I've met some who have given up writing altogether because they can't deal with rejections. That's flight.

Every author will face criticism and rejection, and because of the nature of the work it can feel very personal and trigger a deep fear of failure. It can make you want to stop like a rabbit in headlights, lash out or run away.

But just because your instinctive reaction to fear might be fight, flight or freeze, that doesn't mean you have to act it out. Shit happens but you can choose how you are going to deal with it.

Choose how you want to respond

Bringing your hidden fears into conscious awareness means you are able to take control. You can see and stop your automatic reactions, make a rational assessment of the situation and choose how you want to respond. You can find ways of reframing the things that spark your fears, and cutting them down to size.

These days, for example, I choose to see every piece of work as part of my development as a writer, and therefore of great value whether it finds a publisher or not. If I get rejections, they feel less important because I'm looking at them in this wider context.

I believe everything I write, if I still care enough about it a few years down the line, will be to some extent recyclable, and I've found this to be true. For example, a book I failed to sell ten years ago, *The Binding*, has recently found a publisher. This is another way of taking the sting out of rejections, making them feel like temporary setbacks rather than final judgements.

If I look at things this way, getting rejections doesn't make me feel anxious, or even particularly upset, and I can carry on moving easily from one project to the next without getting bogged down in fear.

Supposing you're held back by fear of feeling exposed in

your writing, being aware of it in your self-talk – 'people will think I'm...' – means you can reframe it. Yes, people will have an opinion about you, but does that really matter?

You could challenge your fear of exposure with the rational argument that we are all flawed and therefore all the same, that our cracks and vulnerabilities are what make us interesting and help other people to relate to us.

You could decide to accept the obvious truth that not everybody in life will like you, but the people who don't like you are not important. In addition to that, if you don't write something because you fear being seen in the writing, then you're also losing out on all the people who might have enjoyed what they read and liked you for writing it.

If you always try to notice your self-talk, press pause on your impulse to fight, flee or freeze and find ways of reframing the things that alarm you so they don't feel alarming any more, over time, your automatic responses change.

You are effectively reprogramming your mind, by blocking off old neural pathways and creating new ones. My old impulse to 'go down the garden and eat worms' has completely gone, as have my fears of responsibility and of feeling exposed.

It does take practice. It's a discipline rather than a once-and-it's-done kind of task. You need to adopt an attitude of vigilance towards your self-talk, to always press pause on gut reactions to fear and remind yourself of the new perspective you're choosing to frame it in.

But it's worth the effort and the added bonus is that learning to tackle fears around your writing in this cognitive way gives you tools for tackling those same fears in other areas of your life.

Summing Up

Knowing what you want to write but not being able to get started is a horrible feeling and it's hard to see anything positive about it, but it may be nature's way of stopping you from starting a project too soon, before you've worked up a proper head of steam.

Or what feels like a block, when you're trying to write but can't seem to find your way in, may simply be part of the creative process; you have to keep calling the muse by showing up every day and making an effort, but she comes in her own time.

If you can't get started even though you have done enough planning and been trying for a while, hidden fears may be holding you back. Fear can be the voice of common sense, but most often it's irrational.

So the questions to consider when you've got an idea but you can't get started are:

- Have you done enough preparation and planning?
- Are you trying to rush the creative process?
- Are there real reasons why the timing or type of project isn't right?
- Could fear be holding you back?

2 When You Still Can't Get Started

If you've done all the preparation and planning you need and begun to root out and challenge any fears that might be holding you back but you still can't get started, don't despair!

There's a tried-and-tested technique for getting the writing flowing again, which also happens to be the 'behavioural' part of the cognitive behavioural therapy approach to tackling fears: just start.

But don't start with the big thing you're stuck on – start small. The idea is fully explored by Susan Jeffers in *Feel the Fear and Do It Anyway*, where she proposes that instead of avoiding the things you find challenging you can build up to confronting them bit by bit.

As your confidence grows and you find you can tolerate feeling a bit scared or uncomfortable, you can gradually build up to the big challenge you have not been able to face head-on.

If, for whatever reason, you can't start the book you really want to write, you may need to break down your block a little at a time, starting with the least challenging kind of writing.

The joy of private writing

The whole point about private writing is that nobody else is ever going to read it, and therefore there is no risk of criticism or rejection, exposure or any of the other things you may be worried about, and you can let go completely of the idea that it has to be good.

This is writing which is completely free, having no association with any particular writing project; it's holistic, designed to help nurture and re-energise your writing self.

> I just get on with some writing – ANY writing – not worrying about how good it is. Short writing exercises can get you back in the mood of writing and, once you've got started, it's much easier to keep the wheels turning.
>
> Liz Kessler

The most well-known approach to creating a practice of private writing is called 'morning pages'. It was described by Dorothea Brande in her wonderful book, *Becoming a Writer*, which was first published in the 1930's and is still in print – that's how good it is. It was later expanded upon for a new generation by Julia Cameron in her mega bestseller, *The Artist's Way*.

Morning pages

The idea is that you write stream of consciousness, whatever comes into your head, for twenty minutes or three pages, not stopping and not censoring yourself. If you run out of ideas, you keep writing anyway, even if it's just, 'I don't know what to write... I think my foot's gone to sleep... what's the point in this?'

Morning pages are ideally done first thing upon waking, before your mind is locked into the concerns of the day.

If writing first thing in the morning is impractical for you, it's better to do it at some stage in the day than not at all, so try to find a time that suits you better and stick to it for a few weeks. If you do your private writing at the same time every day you're less likely to forget.

Similarly, if twenty minutes feels too long, ten minutes a day may suit you better. Experiment with it to find your own best way.

I've met lots of writers who swear by morning pages, either as a long-term practice or for a couple of weeks to get the creative juices flowing again.

But not everyone likes them. Some people find that without any focus or direction they tend to keep going back to the same themes, which are often their pet worries, preoccupations and complaints, so the practice can gradually turn into a sucking vortex of gloom.

For those people, the best way forward with free writing may be to make it just a little bit less free by using writing prompts. Here, you're still writing anything that comes into your head without stopping or censoring, but it isn't completely unfocused; you are writing on a theme.

There are loads of books and websites that offer daily prompts but I think the best prompts are ones you find for yourself.

Writing from prompts

Write a list of headings such as activities, objects, kinds of weather, foods, places... Don't over-think it. Then under each heading write three things, not sifting and selecting but going with your first ideas.

These may be general, particular but not within your personal experience, or situations from your own life, for example, 'Weather – global warming, the California drought, the time I got sunburn in Tiree.' They can be whatever comes into your head.

When you make lists in this way, every item on them will have resonance for you right now because they have emerged spontaneously from your own unconscious.

Choose one thing from one of your lists and write about it for ten minutes, just seeing where the writing takes you. Then write for another five minutes, saying whatever it is that you haven't said.

Writing prompts don't have to be objects or themes. You can create other starters from your thoughts, feelings and experiences such as 'I remember... I wish... I believe' or 'I'm happy when... I'm angry when... I'm sad when...'

You can steer your daily writing towards fiction and fantasy by creating prompts starting with 'What if?' What if Prince Harry went missing? What if winters got colder and longer until, one year, Spring never came? What if some children found a secret door?

You can give your daily writing a positive steer by focusing completely on life-enhancing things, making it a gratitude journal for example, where your prompt is something you feel grateful for each day. You can use a motivational book such as Stephen R Covey's *The Seven Habits of Highly Effective People* to prompt your daily writing.

You can find your prompts in poems you love, or characters and settings in books; TV shows you love or hate, celebs and public figures. Anything that provokes an emotional response in you will be easy to write about.

You don't have to try all these ideas, or feel you have to vary the kind of private writing you do. Private writing is about freedom and spontaneity; doing whatever you fancy will be the best way to find the best writer you can be.

As you develop your practice, you discover where your interests lie in the topics you have chosen, whether it's the inner world of thoughts and feelings or the outer world of facts and information. You hear your unique voice, which may be lyrical or contemplative or practical or funny, as you explore the themes and objects that have sprung spontaneously from you, asking for your attention.

With all your free writing, whether you prefer the unfocused approach of morning pages or the more focused daily prompts, you can enhance the experience by reading back through and underlining a few words and phrases that catch your attention.

This sharpens your awareness of what's going on in your writer mind, and also can provide new prompts for the following days, so that you carry the theme on and explore it more deeply.

The crucial thing is to keep the critical mind out. Free writing has to be whatever comes into your head and if you do it often you soon begin to feel its rhythm and spaciousness, like a breathing in and a breathing out of the mind.

If you don't take to free writing, it might be that the traditional daily practice of keeping a diary will suit you better. Again, you can be flexible and experiment with different ways of doing it.

Keeping a diary

I recommend using a normal notepad rather than a diary with regular sections because you may not want to write every day and you certainly won't have the same amount to say every day.

Your diary could be a straightforward account of the events of your life, or it could also explore your thoughts and ideas. You could include descriptions of places or people you've seen, reports of conversations you've had or overheard, reviews of books you've read or films you've watched, so that your diary becomes in part a writing journal, where some items aren't included because they're telling the story of your day but because they've caught your attention as a writer.

You could theme your diary, so that rather than reading like an autobiography , recounting what happens in general, it reads like a themed memoir, focusing on your thoughts, feelings and experiences around a particular area of interest such as cooking or gardening.

With my own daily practice, I like to mix things up. It started as a dream diary more than forty years ago, just a record of my dreams scribbled in thin, red, floppy-backed exercise books, like the ones I had once used in school.

As I learned more about dreams, I moved to bigger A4 loose-leaf pads and started to record my dreams on one half of the page, leaving the other half free for notes about what was going on in my waking life. So, for a long time, I had two diaries side by side; one of my deep inner world and one of my life in the world above.

Gradually, I added drawings and diagrams, observations and ideas, thoughts on books I was reading, poems. If I thought of something when I was away from home, I'd jot it down on a piece of paper and stick it into my journal when I got back.

I'm not a three pages or twenty minutes a day kind of person; that sort of discipline makes me feel constrained. I like the freedom to write whatever and whenever I want, but that turns out to be most days because I love doing it.

These days, I start each New Year with a brand new beautiful hard-backed A4 notebook and begin recording with a few summarising thoughts about the previous year's private writing.

Like any daily practice, such as yoga, meditation or walking, you have to enjoy your private writing and feel its benefits or you won't keep it up. In order to enjoy it, you need to experiment and find out what works best for you.

At different times, different approaches might work better, so it's good to come to it with an open mind and remain open to all possibilities. Allow your private writing practice to change and develop.

When your life is hectic and demanding you might enjoy the structure of three pages a day, for example, but when everything feels less pressured and your mood is more relaxed and expansive, that discipline may feel like an unwelcome and unnecessary constraint.

Private writing is practice. It's where you can experiment and hone your skills, the way musicians and footballers do in practice and training. Trying to write only for publication would be like a concert musician only picking up their instrument on performance nights, or a footballer only putting on his boots for championship matches.

But more than anything else, private writing reminds you of the reason you want to write in the first place – for the pleasure it brings.

I think for me the main thing about writing, like any activity I am going to give precious moments of my life to, is to become conscious of what it brings me. Once I'm driven internally, nobody can take it away from me. The risk otherwise is it gets all muddled up with 'oughts' and 'shoulds' and vulnerability around self-image and whether people like you and how little you earn.

Moira Munro

With private writing you can take your time and go wherever it leads. You can experiment and play, like a small child, completely absorbed and in the flow. You can explore and discover the richness of your inner life from which all your writing projects spring.

And when you have a particular project in your mind, the book you can't get started on, everything you write in your journal will be somehow connected with it, the way that dreams are connected to waking life.

So private writing doesn't only nurture you as a writer but also, in an indirect way, brings you towards the point when you are ready to make the next step, and do what you could not approach head-on – begin your first draft.

And so to the first draft

One of the things that holds writers back from starting a new project is the notion that the first draft is the book, but the first draft is only part of the process. It's an experiment to see how and whether your idea will work.

The aim of the first draft is simply to find a structure that hangs together and a strong voice, both of which emerge through the writing, so you always have to redraft, and often rewrite whole sections, in the light of what you didn't know when you started.

You should come to the first draft in the same spirit as you come to private writing, like a child at play, because effectively you are only writing it for yourself. No one will read it until you have honed and redrafted with the reader in mind.

Dorothea Brande says there should be two people in a

writer – the child and the adult, the artist and the critic, and the first draft belongs to the child. At the first stage, the most important thing is to keep the critic out.

This can be hard because most of us are taught creative writing the wrong way round, starting by studying techniques and then trying to apply them. Through school and university, we learn to read with an analytical eye so that we can judge what is 'good' and 'bad'. We are graded on our work, as if a story can be measured in an objective way.

This approach is all about training the inner critic, and the upshot is that many of us, by the time we're grown up, believe we aren't creative at all and should leave that sort of thing to others who are. We become consumers of creativity rather than creators.

You do need the critical mind as well as the creative, the adult as well as the child, the craftsman as well as the artist. But the critic's time is after the first draft is finished, and letting it in before that can stop you from starting anything at all.

Art doesn't come from technique; technique develops out of making art. Writing starts from the stories and ideas that fire the writer's soul and it's through the writing that the writer finds and develops his or her own voice.

So let go of the idea that the first draft has to be good. Treat it as a voyage of discovery, and embark upon it in a spirit of openness and curiosity. Whatever happens to your story in the end, the first reason for writing is to please yourself.

Summing Up

If you're stalled before you start with a new idea, you can get the creative juices flowing and build up to it gradually by doing some private writing.

It's a small step from doing private writing to beginning your first draft because nobody will read your first draft either; it will always need redrafting.

Private writing is good practice anyway because it:

- helps you develop your writing voice
- connects you with the themes, stories and objects of your inner world
- reminds you of the pure pleasure of writing.

Start now!

Write stream of consciousness for five minutes, beginning 'When I am not writing...' After that, write for another three minutes, saying whatever it is that you haven't said yet.

Then if you haven't got one already, go out and buy yourself a beautiful writing journal and stick it in.

3 When You Can't Keep Going

So you've been teetering on the edge, dipping the toe, and you've finally taken the plunge. You're writing strongly and happily on the crest of your wonderful idea when, suddenly or gradually, you run aground.

You've got a chapter under your belt, or maybe five chapters, or seven; maybe you're three-quarters of the way through the book, but you've slowed down or stalled and you're thinking about giving up.

The problem with starting to write your book instead of just fantasising about it is that you will soon get a much better idea about whether or not it will actually work. And sometimes it won't.

If you think the idea hasn't got legs, let it go. Put it aside. You can always come back to it later and see if anything can be retrieved and used again.

The same thing applies if you still think the idea will work but you've discovered you aren't that keen on writing it – just let it go. It hasn't been a waste of time because the experience has contributed to your development and self-knowledge as a writer.

After plotting the whole book out and knowing that it all hung together, I still couldn't make myself start writing it. Then I suddenly realised it just wasn't the sort of book I wanted to write, and no matter how hard I tried, if my heart wasn't in it, it would never work. Instead I came up with a completely different idea for a book I really did want to write, and wrote that. Result: one happy writer (and hopefully one successful book!).

Lynne Benton

If you can't see the way forward in the current format, again, let it go, see if you can come at it from a different angle.

Supposing you find, once you start writing, that you're more interested in the ideas and themes than the story, maybe your book will work better as non-fiction. Or if you're more interested in one of the minor characters, who is a child, could your story work better as a children's rather than an adults' novel?

Being able to let go of ideas that don't work or don't fire you is essential to your writing happiness. You aren't likely to make a fortune from your writing, so if it doesn't make you feel good, what's the point in doing it?

But do bear in mind that although thinking your idea isn't good enough or doesn't really fire you after all could be a rational assessment, it could also be a mask for fear, especially if starting projects only to abandon them is a bit of a pattern for you.

Notice what other things you are thinking besides 'it's not good enough' or 'this isn't really doing it for me'. See if a fear of failure, or exposure, or responsibility, or anything else is somewhere in the mix.

Identifying your fears means you can see more clearly whether there is a real problem with the idea or whether your disengagement is emotionally driven.

When you're aware of your fears, instead of automatically reacting by giving up (flight), doggedly refusing to give up (fight) or feeling stuck (freeze), you can make a conscious decision about how you want to move the situation forward.

Getting all your what-ifs out the way means you can concentrate on the creative challenge. If you take away the possibility that your book might shock or upset some people, say, or that the subject might be 'too niche for the market' or that the writing will really stretch you, you might find that the idea itself still feels intriguing and you still want to write the book.

The most common creative problem if you get stuck during the first draft is that the inner critic has got in under the radar before you're ready for it.

Check you haven't lost that relaxed, playful, inquisitive mindset you needed in order to get started. Remember the child is in charge, not the adult; the artist, not the critic, right through to the end of the first draft.

The first draft is an experiment, so expect the unexpected. With non-fiction, you might find that your initial approach is beginning to feel constraining, while a different angle is opening up.

Say you're writing a chronological account of the history of psychology, for example, you might discover that what interests you most is the people behind it, and begin to re-envisage your book as a series of linked biographies.

When you start again from that angle, maybe you'll find you don't want to write them in a purely factual way, but make them opinion pieces, allowing your own views to be heard.

There isn't one definitive best way of writing anything,

so be flexible at this stage; play with different versions and let the book gradually show you what it wants to be.

With fiction, as your characters become more rounded and real, it isn't only up to you how the story unfolds; sometimes, it's up to them.

> There are characters you invent and then they thank you by doing something totally unplanned and ruining your plot.
>
> Rosie Rushton

If you're a planning kind of writer, you might find this unsettling, and your block might come from feeling that you're starting to lose your way. If you like to stick to your original plan, you might need to remind yourself of the details and get your story back on track.

If you're not the kind of writer who likes to follow a detailed plan, some of the excitement of writing fiction is that it can go in unexpected directions and you might have to stop and consult your map even more, to work out whether your current route can ever get you to your destination, or indeed whether you still want it to end up where you originally intended.

Whatever your natural approach, you have to stop and take your bearings from time to time, and you know when because the writing starts to falter. You may have strayed into a side alley that's taking you too far away from the main plot, for example. Then you will need to track back, discarding the last chunk of writing and picking the story up at an earlier point.

You may have thought of a much more intriguing

outcome as you write your way in to the story, and need to rethink your whole plan.

It's hard, but you have to be flexible and willing to make necessary changes as you go along, even if they require a lot of work, or else these checks and pauses which are a natural part of the creative process can turn into major blocks.

Another part of the natural process of the first draft is that it's uneven; there will be parts that feel slow, so you might drag your heels and not really want to engage. The tension always needs adjusting in the redrafting process, once you've found a story structure you can work with.

If your reason for feeling you don't want to go on is because you feel bogged down and you're losing momentum, there are two ways of keeping going. You can either set your shoulder to the wheel and push through to the next exciting bit, or you can skip ahead and backfill later if you need to.

Some authors always write the big exciting scenes first, like a line of stepping stones, and then go back and join them up.

I almost always hit a brick wall in the middle of a project. I think it's about momentum – I love starting a book, and finishing one, but any new idea feels better than being in the middle of a book. I get round it by calculating how many words I have to do per day to meet a deadline (impose one on yourself if you don't have one!) and wading through it, knowing I'll have to edit. Another trick is to go to a scene you feel excited about writing, skipping any makeweight ones in the middle. Often you don't need the scenes that you didn't fancy writing!

Kate Harrison

If you've started but you're struggling with the writing, check that:

- your idea is strong enough
- you aren't being held back by hidden fears
- your inner critic hasn't got in too soon
- you aren't trying to avoid making necessary adjustments
- you aren't getting bogged down by the less dramatic bits.

Then, if you still feel stalled, it's probably because you either don't know enough or you don't care enough to keep going.

Do you know enough?

Although your idea might have felt sufficiently ready for you to get started, you may need to do a bit more research and development once the writing is under way.

For example, in one story I wrote years ago the protagonist was in a wheelchair. A few chapters in, I saw an even more exciting plot possibility than my original idea, but I didn't know whether it would be physically possible. So I had to stop writing and find some wheelchair users with first-hand experience who could advise me.

Your story may have stalled because you don't know

enough about peasant life in eighteenth century France or office politics in the 1940s, modern police procedures or whatever world the action of your story takes place in.

As well as practical difficulties such as not knowing what is physically or perhaps socially possible for your protagonist, gaps in your understanding of their situation are gaps in your understanding of them. If you don't know enough about their situation, you can't really know how they will feel and respond to events.

Settings

The story you tell is the tip of the iceberg; what balances and holds it up is the much bigger part that your reader never sees. You need to know far more about your settings than the details you use in your story, because your characters' lives and motivations spring from their physical and social environment.

So if you've stalled, take some days out to immerse yourself in the settings of your story, ideally by visiting the places where your story is set.

When it isn't possible to physically go, because your story is set in Turkmenistan or the Arctic tundra, say, or even in Manchester or the Scilly Isles if you're strapped for cash and can't afford the fare, or your own home town three hundred years ago, look for books and films set in those times and places, and have a good search for information online.

If your story is set on the planet Xargo or in a post-war London under German rule or in the future then take some proper time to go there in your imagination.

Immersing yourself in your settings

However you research your settings, in the flesh, in books and films or in your imagination, take your time. Pause frequently to take your bearings and notice all the detail in your surroundings.

Use your senses to really get the experience of being there. Savour the quality of the air, the smell of blossom or traffic, the sounds of birds or music, the colours and patterns, the feel of the ground beneath your feet.

It can help to find some pictures or symbolic objects that will remind you of being in the places you've visited for research, so you will only have to see or touch them to be transported back there.

When I was writing my Young Adult novel, *Drift*, I made a collage of the protagonist's suburban world, including some iconic London landmarks, to help me be there even though I was writing in a tiny village on the edge of a Cornish moor.

When I was writing my children's novel, *The Binding*, which is set on a remote Scottish island, I had a group of beach stones and fishing floats on my table that I had picked up on holiday in the far North of Scotland.

As well as the situations and settings of your story, the parts of your protagonist that show are only the tip of the iceberg. You need to know much more about them than the reader does.

Characters

If you feel stalled in your writing, it may be that you don't know enough about your protagonist to be able to tell how he or she will react in a given situation, what their main drives are, what they really want and how far they are willing to go to get it.

> With my second novel I was really blocked in the middle. I knew how the novel ended – about the last third – but how to get there? I became increasingly anxious and frustrated. Then I calmed myself and began to think about the characters. What were their motives, their hopes and desires and what would they be willing to do to attain them? Then the plot fell into place. Now I plan a bit more at the start and always fall back on this if I'm stuck.
>
> Patricia Elliott

Getting a better understanding of your characters is a different kind of research – they are creatures of your imagination and that's where you have to go to find them.

Again, approach it with a child's mind; be open and curious. Let go of what you think you know about your characters; let them surprise you. If you can't progress your story within the limits of what you already know about your characters, you need to find out more.

There are lots of ways you can imagine your characters more fully and get more clarity about what they look like, how they think and feel and their essential nature and spirit.

Characters – get under their skin

To get a deeper sense of their physical presence pretend to be them, the way children pretend to be heroes from films and video games in the playground. Feel what it feels like to be in their physical body. Imagine your face is their face; experience their range of expressions.

Take a step back and imagine you're watching your protagonist on the big screen, playing out one of the scenes in your story. Really see their features; hear the sound of their voice.

Take your time with this. If you do it before you go to sleep, when your mind is relaxed, you may well find that you go on to dream about them too. This can work particularly well with a daytime power-nap.

The best way to get to know someone better in real life is to have a conversation with them. Think about where you might arrange to meet your main protagonist, and set up a meeting in imagination.

Ask what you want to know

Close your eyes and take a few slow breaths, to settle your mind and sink into your inner space. Imagine your protagonist is coming to meet you, and you are waiting for him or her to arrive.

Where are you? Use all your senses to be in your arranged meeting place; notice the general ambience and then focus down into the detail. What can you see, smell, hear, taste, touch?

How does the protagonist look when he or she arrives? What are they wearing? What kind of mood are they in?

Start with small talk, asking them what their favourite food is, their favourite colour, the person they'd most like to meet.

Dig a little deeper, and ask what makes them feel angry and how they would like to be remembered after they're gone.

Find out something about their past. What's their earliest memory? Who was their best friend at school? When did they move to the city?

Some people suggest a whole list of stock questions but I think you should be led by what you personally want to know. You'll want to ask different people different things, the same as in real life. Follow your curiosity.

And don't stick to what seems relevant to your story. Imagine you're chatting with your protagonist in a general kind of way. Character doesn't come from plot; it's the other way around, so knowing more about your protagonist than you think you need for your story is one way of finding out what they're going to do next.

You don't need to write all this down. Imagine the conversation as if it's happening in real life – you wouldn't take note of every single thing someone said to you over coffee or a meal, so just be attentive and notice the things you find particularly interesting or revealing.

Besides chatting with your characters, you can find out more about their attitudes, tastes and feelings by pretending you are them and making a collage.

Be them, see them

Prepare by getting into character. Imagine you are your protagonist, get under their skin. Feel yourself in their body; be in the settings of your story.

Now, as your character, flick through some old magazines, tearing out any images, colours, words or patterns that appeal to you.

Do this without thinking, but just feeling like your character. Don't wonder why this image, why this word, or how it's all going to fit together.

You need a time limit to help you keep this quick and instinctive, because if it's open-ended you can easily become more selective and analytical, so stop after ten minutes.

Then get a large sheet of paper and a glue stick and

make your collage, setting a time limit of five minutes. Stick the torn-out pieces down in any order you like, not worrying about making a coherent picture. Don't feel you have to use them all.

When you've finished sit back and take an overview of your collage. Working as your protagonist, what dominant colours did you choose? Is your collage more indoors or out-of-doors, more man-made or more natural? Is there a dominant element – water, air, fire or earth?

Notice how many people are in your collage, and who they are. Their expressions and body language, their clothing.

Are there any words on your collage? If so, what do they say about your protagonist? If not, what does that tell you about him or her?

Check the details for further clues. There might be a box of chocolates that suggests a sweet tooth, for example, or a monkey that suggests a playful side.

Finally, consider the way the collage is put together. Are the images evenly spaced? Are they organised in lines or areas? Is there a lot of clear space between them, or none at all? Is it all neatly contained within the sheet of paper, or do the images overlap the edges?

Your collage will give a strong sense of what kind of person your protagonist is, what's important to them and where they feel at home. It may also offer specific details that you can use in your story.

Perhaps, for example, there's a building in your picture that you could use as your protagonist's house, or a car that could be their car. There could be a specific item like a piece of jewellery or a book that might either contribute to the scene setting or play a part in the plot.

When I make a character collage I usually stick it on the wall near my desk where I can look at it in idle moments and I find that, over time, more and more is revealed.

As well as getting a clearer idea of your characters' physical presence and how they think and feel, you can deepen your understanding by trying to capture their essential self, or spirit.

The furniture game

One way of capturing a character's essential nature is through the 'furniture game'. Here you're conjuring symbols to express the non-quantifiable essence of your character, which is hard to put into words.

If your character was a piece of furniture, what would they be? Answer off the top of your head, the first thing that comes into your mind, not rationalising it in any way.

Say your character is a table – what kind of table? Find a few words to describe it. There's a big difference between a solid farmhouse table that has family and community gathered around it every day and a delicate antique side-table with a wonky leg.

Now do the same thing with some other questions such as, if your character was a kind of weather, what would they be? An article of clothing, a piece of music, an animal, a colour, a kind of food...

It doesn't matter what questions you choose, just find a dozen or so, and see how quickly a picture develops.

Another way of uncovering the character's essence is through imagining them in early childhood, before life shaped and moulded them into who they are now.

The child is father to the man

Imagine you are your character at the age of about four or five.

Think of your favourite place to play, maybe your grandmother's garden or your bedroom, the school playground, the patch of wasteland at the end of your bombed-out road.

Now, using your non-dominant hand, draw a picture of yourself in that place, playing. Add the background detail, and anyone else who's with you, whether you want them to be there or not.

When you've finished, still using your non-dominant hand, write your (character's) name at the bottom, and any other words you want to put.

If you haven't tried drawing and writing with your non-dominant hand before you might be surprised by how immediately it takes you into the mind of a child.

Finally, think about how the characters all relate to each other in the story. Who is important to each of them? Who is close? What is the nature and history of each relationship?

See your characters in relation to each other

An easy way to explore this is through using small, varied objects such as buttons. If you don't have a button box, any bunch of small objects will do. Gather a whole lot together so that you have a good variety – a silver ring, a pebble, an old penny, a champagne cork, a walnut, a daisy...

Choose one object or button to represent your main protagonist and place it on the table in front of you. Then choose another object or button to represent another of the main characters, and place it somewhere in relation to the protagonist.

Do this with each of the main characters, taking into account, as you place them, where they are in relation to the protagonist and also to each other. You may have to move some that you've already placed in order to accommodate each one in a way that feels right.

Now you have an overview of all the relationships as well as a sense, from your choice of objects, of what each character is like.

The better you know your characters, especially the main protagonist, the more easily you will find your plot, because plot comes from character and not the other way around.

Plot

The most common way you lose momentum in a plot is by letting the focus stray too far from the main protagonist or viewpoint character. Their needs and desires, their struggles and setbacks are the main thrust of the story; they are what draws the reader in and holds her right through to the final page.

The basic story is nearly always this: someone wants something. They try to get it, fail, try again, fail again, keep trying. Often the shape is the 'magic three' – the protagonist tries something but fails, that's the initial event. They try again and fail again, that creates the pattern. The third time, they try and succeed, and the pattern is broken.

Every time they fail, the stakes are raised because their failure has made the situation worse.

Say your hero is being held against his will. He manages to climb out of the window but his captors bring him back. Now his situation is even worse because they have boarded the window up, so his one obvious means of escape is no longer possible and what's more, he's also being held in the dark. What can he try next?

Every door that closes is another opportunity gone, and so the net tightens and the protagonist's chance of getting what they want seems slimmer.

From an emotional viewpoint too, every failure means the protagonist reaches a lower ebb and has a steeper psychological climb back up, if they're going to be able to try again.

Sub-plots have a similar structure, but spring from the other main characters around the protagonist, so you have to really know them too. What do they want? How far are they willing to go to get it?

The end of their story will come just before the end of the main protagonist's. You can use all or any of the same techniques to get to understand your secondary characters better so that you know what their journey and the end of it will be.

Plot comes from characters, so that's where to look if you're stalled with your story. But however strong your plot is, it won't hold your interest long enough to do the work of writing unless you really care what happens to them.

Do you care enough?

You could put your protagonist in the most desperate situation, such as needing a life-saving transplant. You could throw all kinds of complications into the mix and make their situation worse and worse.

A donor has been found, but the transplant fails. Another donor is found, but your protagonist's condition has deteriorated and he's no longer a suitable recipient. But there's a new experimental drug available...

If you don't care about the protagonist, it doesn't matter how much you throw at them, there won't be any tension in the plot. If you don't care, you won't be able to make your reader care either, and they'll soon stop reading and look for something else that feels more interesting.

Creating a protagonist you care about

What makes us care about our characters? Part of what makes them likeable is their flaws and failings. People are complicated, and it's their complications that make them interesting.

Maybe your dying protagonist has done something terrible in the past and is overcome by remorse. He doesn't feel he deserves to be chosen before other people on the list, but he desperately wants to find the person he's hurt and try to make amends.

Now there's more than just the survival instinct at play; there's an extra reason why this person wants to live and more at stake if they die.

Think about your protagonist's higher motivations. Retribution is important to everyone because everyone can be wronged. A passion for justice, a love for nature, a belief in friendship, family loyalty, the protection of the weak – these values matter to all of us, and if they drive your protagonist in some way, then we are all invested in their story.

Think about their struggle to triumph over adversity, and how this might be felt as an archetypal struggle of good against evil. Can you make the lightness lighter and the darkness even darker?

Intensify the conflict, and remember that inner conflict can be an even greater source of tension than conflict between the self and others. Crank that up too.

Finding the story that matters

There may be occasions when you find, in the writing, that what you thought you cared about doesn't really matter any more, because some other part of the story feels more interesting. Then you may want to refocus your story, to centre on the part you care most about.

For example, as you explore and develop the situation of your protagonist, Harry, who is struggling to decide between his wife and his lover, you might find the character you're most interested in is the wife, who has a secret of her own.

If she is the most interesting character, the one you really care about, the book might flow more easily if you made it her story.

Sometimes, rather than feeling more invested in another character than your protagonist, you may discover that you still love your protagonist but the issue they're facing doesn't matter as much as something else that comes up in the course of the writing.

Supposing the book you planned was about an obese woman who wants to get fit enough to run the London marathon. In the course of her trying to lose weight you might find out what started her compulsive eating disorder in the past, and that might be a much more interesting story than her quest to run the marathon.

Again, you may want to re-centre your story around the part that feels most important and engaging, that you care much more about.

Sometimes the story starts developing in a way you didn't expect, but which feels more exciting than your original concept. You might set out to write a fantasy novel with vampires but find that the relationship between the main characters is becoming so compelling that the fantasy element feels like a distraction, or even an irritation. You might want to drop the vampires and write it as a real-life romance.

When your first draft falters because your interest in the story that you planned is flagging, identify who and what you care about most in it, regroup and follow your heart.

A change is as good as a rest

Gathering new information about your settings and characters, and making sure you care enough about them to go the hard yards of writing their story, means going back to the drawing board.

Embrace it. When you can't keep going, step away from the computer and enjoy a spot of pondering. Just like when you can't get started, this is a time for patience.

> Almost every novel I've written has had very sticky patches when I've thought I couldn't get through. Sometimes I think it's a bit like childbirth, a pain you have to get through and some babies are more painful than others! But for me the solution always comes down to walking – walking on my own, and letting myself think. Not staring at the screen, that's for sure.
>
> Nicola Morgan

You might find that even when you've sharpened up the characters, refocused the action and immersed yourself in the settings, you still need time away from the book to let the new information sink in before you're able to get writing again.

Take a couple of days or weeks, or even months if you need to. From a distance of several weeks, you'll be more able to see the big picture and the way ahead will look much clearer.

Seeing the big picture can be a problem when you're writing non-fiction as well as fiction, and the solution is the same: step away from it for a while. The temptation is to keep doing more and more research, because there's a chance that something you read might give you a flash of inspiration about how to move forward with your own book.

But endless research, far from helping you to find a structure that works, can actually create more complications and confusion. If you're sufficiently interested in a subject to have started trying to write a book about it, you probably already know a fair bit and, once you've decided on the shape and scope of your book, you can top up your knowledge as you go along, on a need-to-know basis.

If you really don't feel you know enough, then 'Do you care enough?' is the key to efficient research, because if you follow your heart, not trying to find out every single thing you possibly can about your subject, but just what really fires your interest, you're already creating an angle and a focus.

Just be aware that although your finished non-fiction book needs to be well researched and verified, getting stuck back into unfocused research when the writing has stalled can be an avoidance tactic, because reading is so much easier than writing.

If you can't bear to be not writing, while your current project is on hold, I recommend thinking about a different one. I find that feeling excited by a new idea helps me to be patient and stay away from the book that's stalled, while it reforms and reorganises itself in the back of my mind.

It also helps me not to feel frustrated when I lose momentum, because a hiccup with one piece of writing is an opportunity for another, and when I go back and finish the first, the second one is waiting.

Having various writing projects on the go at the same time, each at different stages of development, creates flow in your writing life. It protects you from feeling down and adrift when you've finished a book and relieves the pressure of waiting for feedback from your focus group, agent or publisher by giving you something else really exciting to think about.

Instead of putting all your focus on one project, which will finish, it lifts the focus to you as a writer and your writing life, which is abundant and continuous, like any other force of nature.

You might say that if you were to leave your work-in-progress and get stuck into something else you would never come back to it. But whilst you aren't actively writing, you are holding your ideas in the back of your mind.

The unconscious mind isn't only the source of all your ideas and imaginings – it is also the home of form. You can only wrestle your plot up to a point. After that, you have to let go and let it grow, all on its own.

If you have done the work of research, and if you care enough, it will. When the new information and ideas have settled and firmed up enough for the next stage of the writing, you will feel ready to get stuck in again.

Summing Up

If you've started writing but are struggling to keep going, the problem might be that your idea really isn't going to work. Before you decide to abandon it, however, check that your decision is not driven by hidden fears.

Make sure your inner critic hasn't got in – remind yourself that the first draft does not have to be good.

Ask yourself:

- Do I know enough?
- Do I care enough?

Gather new information, especially about your protagonist and then, if necessary, give it time to ripen and settle before you try to start writing again.

4 When You Get Completely Stuck

But what if nothing works? You've managed to get started, you've tried to keep going, but you feel completely stuck. You're beyond trying; you've hit the wall.

Or what if you can keep going but you really don't want to, because the pleasure's gone out of it and it just feels like a slog?

When you seriously question whether you can go on being a writer, or whether indeed you want to, it feels like an existential crisis, because that's what it is. Being a writer isn't a job or a hobby; it's who and what we are.

But the function of a crisis is to produce necessary change. The change you need might indeed be to give up writing, but it's more likely that you've got out of balance as a writer and need to find your equilibrium again.

Breathe in, breathe out

Creative work is a combination of inspiration and realisation. Inspiration means literally 'breathing in', and realisation means making real in the outer world.

Inspiration is the magic, the mystery, the surprising objects springing from the unconscious as if we were dreaming awake. Inspiration requires stillness and openness, a listening and receptive mind, whereas realisation requires work and practical effort, a focused and active mind.

Too much inspiration and too little realisation means you may have a constant and overwhelming flow of brilliant ideas but never actually write a book, or write books that are half-baked and not as good as they could be.

Too much focus on productivity can mean the joy and magic get lost; ideas may feel harder to come by and less compelling, so that you lose interest in them and don't want to follow them up.

Each book begins with a flash of inspiration and goes on to become a to-and-fro process of daydreaming and focus, receptiveness and effort. We have an idea, write some notes; ponder, walk, dream; write some more notes.

We make some kind of plan, start writing, stop to regroup, sit in cafes, daydream. Adjust our plan and start writing again.

Sometimes, the receptive phase will come in a long ponder and produce a detailed plan, so there's less stop-start in the writing process. Other times, you may need to begin every chapter or section with a spell of stillness as your ideas firm up in your mind.

Every writer has their own natural rhythm, as does every piece of writing, but it always involves inspiration and realisation – breathing in and breathing out. Quite often, when we think we're blocked, we're simply in the receptive phase, and need to be more patient.

The problem is that in our culture we don't value stillness and receptivity; we only value busyness and productivity. Have you noticed that if you ask someone how they are, they will usually reply 'keeping busy' or 'very busy' as if busyness is a measure of well-being?

Busyness is also how we measure our self-worth; not being busy offends our ideas about how we should be, and the notion that results can come from doing nothing offends our ideas about how life ought to be.

We want productivity to reflect the hours we put in at the computer and expect to be able to produce books like sausages, one after the other, so long as we apply ourselves to it.

The publishing business supports our cultural assumptions and values, with schedules for productivity, one book a year, two books a year, or as was once suggested to me, a series of twelve books at a production rate of one every two months.

This may be possible for some writers, especially if they're comfortable with the commercial model of becoming a 'brand' and sticking to writing the same kind of books, but it isn't possible for all of us, and even someone who has been happily churning out three books a year for a decade can suddenly run out of steam.

Just as each piece of writing goes through a process of receptive and active phases, so does each writer. After a productive period we may need fallow time, when we're not thinking about writing at all, a time of total rest and recovery.

I know some writers like to catapult themselves into the next project, but that's not how it works for me. I like the space. I want to sit in it a while, remind myself how it feels, gaze out the window without any intention, and I want to do the things I love doing but haven't had time to do. Writing is not always very inclusive, is it? It's like an overgrown leylandii and tends to get a bit out of control and shut out everything else.

Abi Burlingham

We may need fallow time, but we don't always want it, because it feels like laziness when we should be getting on, and it's getting in the way of what we want. But if we try to fight it, we can't win, because we're fighting against nature, and nature will have its way.

When we need to stop but refuse to give in, sooner or later life will take away the choice. Then we may sink into depression, becoming incapable of action or achievement, so that all we can do is detach and be still.

So many creative people suffer from periods of depression that it almost feels like part of the creative process. Whatever else is going on in your life that seems to be the cause, one of the effects may be to deliver a necessary winter of frozen inactivity if we don't willingly surrender to our need for fallow time.

Depression is a bleak and terrifying darkness, but if we let go of our ideas about how things ought to be and what we ought to be achieving, what we want and think we need, in short, if we let go of our ego-needs, this sinking down into the depths of self can be a fruitful darkness.

Being able to stop when we need to instead of battling on gets easier with experience because it works. Taking time to build new energy and ideas means that when you're back in the writing zone again the work flows much more quickly and easily.

Taking fallow time to rest can actually produce a boost in productivity and even if you've got a deadline and feel you can't, mustn't, won't stop bashing your head against the brick wall of your block, your unconscious mind knows about your deadline; it will use the focus to bring you back more or less in time, even if you need to ask for an extension. It's rare for an author to have a deadline and fail to deliver at all.

Finding your rhythm, letting go when you need to, not trying to bend your writing to your will, is a more efficient and productive approach than trying to force it, and it's also more enjoyable.

If you are completely stuck and feel you can't or don't want to go on, then simply stop. Let go. Surrender. Pay attention to your thoughts and feelings, letting them be what they will be, not expecting or requiring anything directly attached to your writing to come out of it.

Free your mind. Breathe in, breathe out. When you are back in balance, your creativity will return.

I'm doing a PhD on my experience of writer's block at the moment. After my fourth published book I suddenly found that I couldn't get my plots to work. Plotting for most writers is an intuitive process; although a plot has an almost scientific logic and authenticity to it, we can only see this pattern in retrospect. Suddenly I couldn't intuit my way any more – all my plots petered out or felt forced. None of my ideas took off.

While researching the creative process I came across a book about Taoism, and was struck by the parallels between attitudes conducive to creativity and attitudes endorsed by Eastern philosophy: non-attachment, mindfulness, choiceless awareness, beginner's mind, not-knowing, and letting go of the ego.

For three years I tried to write, and at the same time explored Eastern philosophy, (including a hard-core ten-day Vipassana meditation retreat at which I sat with my legs crossed for ten days straight!). It was only when I accepted failure, let go of my current project, and surrendered to the fact that maybe I should do something else with my life, that my creativity returned – almost overnight. I'd suggest that it is only by letting go of expected outcomes and egoic desire that we can be truly creative – a point of view which would seem to contradict the values of an increasingly aspirational and acquisitive Western culture.

Heather Dyer

Fallow time is a chance to regenerate. You always come out of it with fresh new ideas, which may be very different from anything you had planned, because always trying to be in control means you're always restricted to what you or your publishers want, whereas writing may have bigger plans for you.

Fallow time is also a chance to re-evaluate. Sometimes losing the ability or the desire to write may mean we have lost sight of what really matters to us as writers, and our current goals are out of sync with our core values.

Are your writing goals in line with your core values?

Your core values are what drive and motivate you, so if your writing goals are aligned with them, they will feel strong and meaningful. If your goals are not in line with your core values, you're less likely to meet them, and if you do meet them you're less likely to feel any great satisfaction.

> I remembered my personal studies of Stevenson, who had always fascinated me. In Samoa he'd written 'heart' stories set on the island, now regarded as some of the best fiction in his cannon, but which his agent had failed to sell at the time. Stevenson retreated somewhat wearily to 'Scots' stories, which would sell, labouring through the beginning of *Weir of Hermiston* before his untimely death. Dictating every day to his step-daughter, Belle, one can sense the struggle to keep going. His Samoan diary records: 'It begins to pall.'
>
> Lesley Howarth

It's very easy to assume that what you want, as a twenty-first century author, is big advances, a high public profile, prizes, book tours and festival appearances, because that's what all authors want, isn't it?

But what if you don't like the idea of being tied into huge multi-book advances, if you feel public appearances are a waste of writing time, if you don't believe that prizes mean anything, and aren't that keen on travelling? Such people do exist. I'm one of them.

I generally know what I want and tailor my goals accordingly, but I still feel the pressure of other people's values at times and agree to do things such as appearing at major festivals, only to remember that it doesn't do anything for me.

If you're completely stuck, it could be a good idea to look at your writing goals and check that they're motivated by your own core values and not other people's. Friends and family, fellow authors, strangers who ask if they should have heard of you, all of them have their own assumptions, which can easily undermine yours.

Some core values never change. They're deeply ingrained in your personality, and will have been visible in you as a child. A delight in art, in nature, in nurturing others. A hunger for adventure, for justice, for knowledge.

I've discovered that one of my main drives in writing, as in life, is that I love a new challenge, and this core value has led to me chasing several completely different writing goals at different periods in my career. As soon as I feel I know how to do something, I want to try something else.

This unshakeable love of the new has shaped my whole career, but the various directions I've taken because of it have been motivated by changes in what felt most important to me at the time, because some values will develop as you gain life experience.

My first ambition was to become a jobbing writer – it was all about learning and earning. I found that working for educational publishers was a perfect fit, but once I felt confident in my writing skills, I began to get restless.

Around that time, I was researching ways of handling

bullying, because one of my children was having problems at school, and that experience led me to feel really strongly that the advice usually given to children was next-to-useless. So my second ambition was to become a children's self-help writer.

I wrote eight children's self-help books and was beginning to feel that I'd said everything I wanted to, when my circumstances changed. I'd discovered that you couldn't earn any kind of living writing trade non-fiction for children, and I needed to earn more money because my marriage broke up.

Not wanting to go back to educational writing, I decided to try my hand at children's series fiction, which the market was very keen on at the time.

After two successful series, I had a big birthday, and my priorities changed again. Suddenly the most important thing seemed to be to get on and write the adult books on dreams and writing that I'd always intended to write one day. That's the goal I'm aiming for at the moment.

Because some values can change with experience, it's good to re-evaluate from time to time. For example, through experience of the creative process we may come to value fallow time where previously we only valued activity and productivity. In that case, we may want a writing career that allows plenty of space for contemplation, rather than a continuous stream of contracts.

Supposing you've decided to learn to write because you want to quit your job and earn lots of money as an author. If that's your main motivation, when you discover that writing is hard, being published even harder, and earning a decent living well nigh impossible, you'll probably give up and look for a different way of getting out of your rut.

But if, in the meantime, through starting to write, you've discovered a passion for writing which has nothing to do with making money, then you might decide to keep writing even though it's unlikely to become a career option.

Your motivation has changed, and your primary goal has also changed in line with it; you still want to learn to write, but your goal is for writing to enrich your current life rather than replace it.

We may not always be aware when our values have shifted, except as a vague feeling that writing doesn't feel as important or exciting as it used to.

We may not notice, either, if our goals have shifted away from what feels most important and meaningful to us personally because of pressure from other people's values.

If you're stuck because you aren't fired by your writing and lack motivation, it's like when your plot has stalled and you don't really know where you're going with it. The key to finding a strong sense of direction in your plot is in the characters, and the key to finding a strong sense of direction in your writing is in you.

You can get new insights into what makes you tick by using similar techniques to ones you might use to get to know your characters better. Here's one I find particularly useful.

What are your core values?

Think of someone you admire. It could be someone famous or someone you know personally, a historical figure or a contemporary. Go with the first person who comes into your mind and write down their name.

Think of three things you like or admire them for, and write those down. Again, the first things that come into your head. Then reduce those down to abstract nouns.

Do this process with two other people you admire.

Repeat the exercise with three people you dislike or don't admire at all.

The first person I thought of as I typed that was Carl Gustav Jung. I'm writing his name even though there are things I don't admire about him because it's important not to analyse and over-think this, and his is the first name that came to me.

What three things do I admire him for? Off the top of my head, I admire him for refusing to be bullied by Freud into accepting his system, for being one of our greatest explorers of dreams and for the round tower he built by hand in his garden.

What universal qualities could those reduce to? I'm going for independence, imagination and practical creativity.

William Blake was the second person who came to mind for me. I love that he developed his own printing system, that he dedicated himself to his work, even though he never sold anything, and that he saw an angel in a tree. Practical creativity, independence, imagination.

My third would have to be Van Gogh. Again, he was devoted to his art despite his complete lack of worldly success, he made a yellow house to welcome his painter friend and he loved the natural world. Independence, practical creativity, love of nature.

When you do this, you may feel a pattern emerging. My three choices were all independent people but not loners – they all depended upon strong social supports, Jung from his family life, Blake from his marriage and Van Gogh from his brother Theo.

I love their independence and dedication to their creative process, but also their connection with other people, and connecting with other people is another strong drive in my writing.

Another thing that strikes me is that mental stability doesn't seem to be something I value very highly, as the last two were both famously flaky and Jung suffered a complete breakdown which was, he said, the source of all his most innovative work.

I should add, before anyone emails me to tell me I've got these people wrong, that it doesn't matter whether what you like about your heroes is based on factual knowledge, because it isn't about them, it's about you. It's *your* core values you're looking for, so what you think you know about them is what matters, not the historical facts.

When I thought about three people I dislike or don't admire at all, the first name that came to me was Sigmund Freud.

The three things I dislike about him are that he thought he knew better than his patients did themselves about their own lives and feelings, he devised a system and stuck to it rigidly, and he tried to bully Jung into accepting it too.

What universal qualities do the things I dislike about Freud reduce down to? I'd say dogmatism, mental rigidity and hunger for power. The other names that have popped into my head in this category are Margaret Thatcher and Tony Blair.

Look back over your notes and see whether certain qualities have come up a number of times. Where they are similar to each other, amalgamate them, so for example, independence, adventurousness and originality scored highly for me, and they're definitely in the same ballpark. So did beauty and creativity, and love and connecting with others.

See if a pattern is emerging. Is anything noticeable by its absence? For me, something that's definitely missing is worldly success, celebrity and status. Those things might be top of your list – every writer is different and there's no best or better way to be.

Your heroes and villains are a true compass of what you most aspire to and what you want to avoid. Another exercise I like involves your personal environment, which can reveal a lot about the things you value most.

Notice your core values in the way you live your life

Think about your home. Start in your living room. Notice the colour scheme and style, the objects and ornaments, the over-all feel of the room and the details. What particular books are in your bookcase? What ornaments on your shelves? How would you describe this room?

Do the same thing for your kitchen and bedroom. Describe each room and then reduce your descriptions to the essence, for example, fashionable, contemporary, neutral, comfortable, expensive, artistic, unusual. What does the environment you feel at home in say about your values?

Think about your personal things, which are private and entirely chosen by you, such as your handbag or briefcase. How would you describe the outside of it? What do you keep inside? What does it say about you?

Another personal space is your computer – what do you enjoy most when you're in there? Do you love networking, blogging, shopping, finding information, listening to music, playing games, keeping up with the news?

You create your own environment to a large extent, and what you choose to surround yourself with reveals a lot about what drives and motivates you.

Finally, think about the things you enjoy. Who do you like spending time with, and why? Think of half a dozen people.

What do you enjoy doing in your free time, and what's so enjoyable about it? What do you think you might enjoy doing if you had more free time? Why do you think you might enjoy it?

What places do you love, or have you loved, visiting? What appeals to you about them?

Thinking about your personal spaces and the things you enjoy, see if any themes are emerging and what is noticeable by its absence.

When you have a clearer picture of your drives and motivations, think about your current writing goals. Do they spring from the things that matter most to you, your core values right now? Or are they going to give you things you don't really want?

Ask yourself, 'If I stick to my current writing goals, what will I gain and lose in the future?'

Then ask yourself, 'When I'm on my deathbed, what will I be glad I've written and sorry that I didn't write?'

This could be the first step in setting new goals, if that's what you need to do in order to get out of your stuck place.

When you're setting new goals, don't limit yourself to what feels realistic or achievable, because that judgement may come from fear of even trying, in case you fail. Think about what you really want, your biggest dreams for yourself as a writer.

Three doors, three writing futures

Jot down a new direction you're tempted to go in, either an individual project you've been thinking about or a new general area such as romantic fiction or children's books.

Close or lower your eyes, take a few slow, easy breaths, and relax into your inner world of imagination. Picture three closed doors in front of you. One goes into your current writing life, one into this new project or direction and the other into a life of not writing at all.

Stand in front of the closed doors for a few moments

before you choose one to go through. Are they all the same, or different from each other?

Choose a door, open it, stand at the threshold and take in the scene. Now go inside and have a good look around. Use all your senses to fully experience this place, which may be a room, or a garden, a landscape, a tunnel – it can be anything you like. Notice how you feel emotionally being there.

Come out and close that door behind you. Take a few breaths and go through the next one. Repeat this with all three doors. Visualisation is a brilliant way of literally seeing how you feel.

You can use this visualisation at any point when you're considering a new project or direction, and looking for your next writing goal. It will show you whether you are going with your heart – which is your core values – or chasing after something you don't really want.

Some of the doors I've chosen not to go through in my career have been becoming a professional expert/speaker/consultant on the back of my self-help books and writing quizzes and practical exercises for inclusion in another author's book.

Both of these opportunities would have been very lucrative. The first would have involved speaking to parents in workplace situations for a fee of a thousand pounds per session and the second would have earned me more for a few short pieces than a whole book I had written myself, because the author was very high-profile and the anticipated sales were huge.

But these opportunities offered things I didn't value and didn't offer the things I did, so they would have been a bad fit for me, and I've never regretted turning them down, although some of my friends thought I was mad.

When you find a new goal that's a good fit for you, the next thing is to make a plan for working towards it.

Plotting a path to success

Start by clearing out all the things you do that won't help you towards this new goal and would be taking up time you could be dedicating to it.

For example, when I set myself my current goal of doing my adult books on dreams and writing, I decided to stop making school visits, which use up a lot of travel time and nervous energy, and quit the team on the children's books blog, Girls Heart Books, where I had been blogging once a month.

When you've cleared some space, write a list of things you could do that would support your new goal, both in your writing and your non-writing life. This might include building an online platform through blogging and connecting with groups and individuals who might be interested in your project.

It might include doing research, going on training days, joining societies that specialise in the area you're working in. And, of course, it will include the actual writing.

If your project is quite niche and might not find a traditional publisher, you might want to add doing some research into self-publishing and joining related networks.

Unless, like me, you're allergic to timetables, you might like to put a time frame on everything, so that you have mini-targets to meet in a step-by-step way and a finish date for completing your book.

The ideas in this chapter are mostly based on life coaching. Not everybody likes working in this kind of way, but if you do I would recommend getting a book that goes into it in much more depth and detail than I can here. My favourite one is by Bekki Hill, *Coach Yourself to Writing Success*.

Or you could actually have some life coaching to help you get on the right track and stay focused. When I did this, I chose an astrological life-coach Pat Neill, and I loved the extra dimension of starting with my birth chart so I could see my natural strengths and weaknesses, the raw material I was working with and where I might come up against problems.

You can also use creative image work to uncover your deepest drives and motivations and check if your current writing goals are in line with them.

What is your purpose?

Sit quietly for a few moments and take three slow easy breaths. Still your mind.

Lower or close your eyes, and move into your inner

space. Ask, 'What is my life's purpose?' and let the question float away as you continue to breathe slowly and easily.

Now think of an object. Accept the very first thing that drops into your mind. Don't judge or analyse it away.

Examine your object from every angle, noticing its particular characteristics.

Ask your object, 'What is your purpose?'

Again, don't rationalise or censor; go with the first answer that pops into your head.

When I did this, I saw an enormous colourful fish, swimming in clear water. I noticed that it was not scary, and that it was on its own, not part of a shoal. It was just a fish in water and yet, because of its size, it seemed remarkable.

When I asked the fish, 'What is your purpose?' I didn't get an answer straight away, so I asked myself, 'What is the purpose of this remarkable fish?' Then I saw that its purpose was to be remarkable!

I live a very ordinary life, yet it feels remarkable to me, as anyone who has close contact with their dreams and imagination will feel their life to be. I am excited by remarkable things.

So in my writing, I don't want to do something I've done before; ideally I don't want to do things anyone has done before. So I'm happiest if I feel I'm breaking new ground, such as with *Bullies, Bigmouths and So-called Friends* ('Could this be the first self-help book for children?' asked the reviewer in *The Independent*) or *Writing in the House of Dreams* ('Why not combine dreams with creative writing?

I don't think that's been done before!' said my friend and fellow author, Joe Friedman).

It doesn't matter whether I actually am breaking new ground in my writing, but I do need to feel that I am. That is what makes writing feel valuable and meaningful to me, and when I stray, I struggle.

Everyone gets fed up and disillusioned with their work from time to time, and all writers have periods when their energy or commitment to writing feels lower than usual. Who hasn't asked themselves what the point is in doing something so hard for such an uncertain return? Who wouldn't sometimes like to throw in the towel and do something easier, or spend more time socialising or seeing the world?

Feeling stuck or dragging your heels, can be par for the course for a couple of days or weeks, especially at times when writing is taking you away from other things you want or ought to do, but if it goes on for a long time, something has to give.

Change is never easy. We try to hold on to the way things are, even when they are not very good, and it can take a real crisis to dislodge us.

If the crisis comes, and you get completely stuck with your writing, the change you need might be no more than taking time away from it, and adopting a more positive attitude towards the important work of daydreaming, pondering and sitting around in cafes that will help you avoid crashing again in the future.

Or it may be that you need to change your writing goals to bring them more in line with your core values, and that could feel particularly unsafe if you are an established writer, because you have more to lose.

Change doesn't only feel risky – it is risky. When you step away from your writing, stop trying to push the river, let go of what you want and think you need, pay attention to your mind without attachment to outcomes, this will almost certainly help you find new energy to re-engage with your current writing goals or find new ones.

But the risk is that if you take time out and re-evaluate your goals, you might discover that you really don't want to write any more, and what would your life be without it?

It's very unlikely that you'll decide the reason you're stuck is because you actually want to stop writing, but it is possible, and if it happens it will be because there are other, different things beginning to feel more meaningful and dynamic to you now.

Impermanence is the nature of being, but when one thing ends, another begins.

I was writing a follow-up to a children's book which hadn't done badly, a romp through time, set in a funeral parlour! A bit of black humour seemed to have been just the ticket for my publisher. But the feeling had been growing upon me for some time, and through several books, that the heart had gone out of it.

At the same time, I'd been studying for a degree in history and literature, and I found that my interest in facts, rather than fiction, had been growing.

As I ploughed on with the sequel to my quirky funeral parlour story, establishing the characters of two eccentric aunts who would be useful in the twists and turns of my rather gothic tale, I found that I was just putting plot points into place. I looked at what I'd written. Did

I care about it? Was it grounded in anything true, or useful? What was it about? The feeling grew more and more leaden.

At last I came to the point which made me think, 'Not one more paragraph. Not one more sentence – not one more word.' I put it away. I knew that, come what may, I wasn't going to write it any more. I fulfilled the contractual commitment by offering a previously published book which had done well, to my publisher – they were quite happy. They didn't pursue my follow-up, and neither did I. For the first time, I didn't cook up new ideas, or synopses. A sense of closure gradually dawned. It felt liberating.

Lesley Howarth

Summing Up

If you reach a crisis point when you feel you can't or don't want to go on with your writing, it doesn't usually mean you need to give up completely; it means you have to change the way you're doing it.

When you feel completely stuck:

- check that you're giving equal importance to the productive and the receptive phases of writing
- accept that you may need fallow time to rest and re-evaluate
- identify your core values
- if necessary, adjust your writing goals to be more in line with your core values.

5 When You're Putting Off Redrafting

You would think that once you'd finished your first draft you should be on the home straight, yet this is the part where I always used to stall. There were two reasons why.

The first reason was that it didn't feel exciting. By the time I had finished the first draft, I knew what the book was, and there was nothing left to discover. The second reason, which I only acknowledged later, was that I didn't really know what I was doing.

The first draft is all about opening up to the unconscious processes, as Dorothea Brande says. It's like dreaming awake and it came naturally to me because when I started writing I had already been recalling and working with dreams for years. I describe the creative approach I developed from dreamwork in *Writing in the House of Dreams*.

But redrafting, although it still draws on unconscious processes and can have the same 'magical' feel, is also about technique. I found the art of writing easy, but I had to learn the craft.

Now that I know how to do it, I still prefer the freedom and excitement of the first draft, but I look forward to redrafting too, because it's a different kind of pleasure.

If you hate rewriting, learn to love it. I always feel a great sense of relief when I have my first draft safely down on paper – well, screen. Every morning after that, I can't wait to get back to it, to shape it and sharpen it, to cut and polish and just generally sparkle it.

Valerie Wilding

The redrafting process is different for everybody, depending upon how you go about writing your first draft. For those who write lean, like me, redrafting usually means putting flesh on the bones, because the first complete draft can feel sketchy and slight.

For those who write long, it's more a question of pruning away the excesses. I heard a prominent author on a book programme recently saying that he thought one reason why traditionally published novels tend to be longer now than they used to is because publishing houses have fewer editors. He said most long novels would be better shorter, and that's something I have often felt myself.

If you tend to redraft as you go along, starting each day reading back over what you wrote yesterday and making amendments, then by the time you've finished the first draft it may already be nearly as good as you can get it, and only need a few tweaks when you come to look back over the whole thing.

If you gallop through, never pausing to check and look back until you reach the end, your redrafting process is likely to be longer.

Whatever your first draft is like, lean or flabby, tidy or sketchy, starting a complete redraft can feel overwhelming.

You might be tempted to tell yourself it's fine, it'll do. I'm afraid it almost certainly isn't, and it won't.

A first draft is a first draft, and if you send it to publishers or go straight to self-publishing, you're not honouring your story in the way it deserves, considering all the time, effort and passion you've put into getting it this far.

If you're serious about writing, you wouldn't want your name to be associated with half-baked, amateurish manuscripts or ebooks, so it's worthwhile both for the book and yourself as a writer, to make sure that nothing goes out with your name on it that isn't the absolute best it can be.

I have to gear myself up to redrafting, so I always set my manuscript aside for a while between drafts. It's hard to see the whole thing anyway, when you're really close to it, so if you possibly can, you should always try and get some distance from it before you start redrafting.

Put your complete first draft on one side and take a break, or work on something different so that you're still in the creative space but not thinking about your draft.

My top tip for redrafting is to leave the book for much longer than is normally recommended. They say a month or six weeks but in my experience I need to put it aside for at least 4 months. This is difficult to do – but it makes all the difference. By that time I really can read it with fresh eyes. Anything less and I can't.

Rosalie Warren

Resting your draft is one way of getting a more objective perspective on it; another way is to seek someone else's views. Some writers like to find a trusted reader at this stage, to help them get a clearer idea of what issues they need to address in redrafting.

But be very careful who you choose. Your book is still young and vulnerable, and a critical reader can easily make you doubt your instincts and interrupt the natural flow for you. On the other hand, an uncritical reader won't give you anything useful and might make you think you don't need to bother with redrafting much at all.

I remember reading some advice on how to pitch your book to agents and publishers which said you should never, ever tell them 'my child/partner/best friend loved it' because that doesn't mean anything, except perhaps that your approach to feedback is sloppy and unprofessional.

I've heard of writers falling out with friends over the reading of manuscripts; the one who has done the reading might feel offended if their advice isn't taken, or the one who has written the manuscript might feel disappointed if it is received with anything less than a hundred per cent enthusiasm.

I even know someone who read for a friend and got sued a few years down the line, because the friend thought she had stolen some ideas from her manuscript to use in her own new book.

This isn't an issue for me personally because I don't like anyone to read my work until I've done multiple redrafts and made it as good as I can on my own. You have to find out by trial and error what works best for you.

If you do decide to show your draft to other people, always remember that it's your project and don't believe that anyone can know what it needs better than you. Use feedback to help you refine your ideas, and only take suggested changes on board if you feel that they will make your book better.

A very good agent or editor or a friend you trust is a good resource. You will know your own feelings much better if they say something you can either agree or disagree with... You'll either feel: WHY didn't I think of that? Or you'll think: This person is MAD and has no idea what I'm trying to do.

Adèle Geras

I think of the first draft as 'finding the lump', digging up the raw piece of stone or wood, or working the rough clay until you can see, in its shape, the beautiful object it has the potential to become.

Redrafting is 'crafting the lump'. It isn't a one-off job, but a process of shaping and re-imagining, of working and whittling, so that the potential you have glimpsed in your raw material becomes something finished and complete, that will be pleasing to others.

There are two main stages in this crafting process. First, you have to take the lump and continue shaping it, knocking off the knobbly bits and filling in the holes, until the basic structure is just right. That is your macro-edit.

Once you've knocked it into shape, you can work on the surface, paying attention to the fine detail in your micro-edit, which we'll go into in the next chapter.

At plot level, be ruthless

Arguably, getting the plot right is the most important part of the redrafting process because publishers and agents normally decide which manuscripts to read based on a synopsis and first chapter.

When you're at the macro stage of redrafting, think big. Having rested your first draft and got some distance on it, come back to it as a reader and read the whole thing right the way through, in a sitting.

Notice where the story grips you and where it seems to lose momentum. Does it draw you in from the very first page? Does it build in intensity, reach an exciting climax and deliver a satisfying ending?

Most first drafts don't, because you need to have the whole story in front of you before you can see how to adjust all its parts in relation to each other.

If your story feels unfocused or saggy in places, if the beginning is slow or the ending flat or hurried, bold action may be necessary. It can feel daunting, but when you embrace the fact that you need to make big structural changes, you might find it's quicker and easier than you think.

Here's my top tip for redrafting: always, always, always work from a copy. Save the current version before you start a new one, so that you still have the original to compare it with and go back to if it turns out the new draft doesn't work as well.

That frees you up to play with different versions and makes even the boldest changes feel less risky

Be brave, be ruthless. If you cut a character or a scene and they really need to be there – they will fight their way back in!

Cas Lester

Most authors who have been traditionally published will have had the experience at some time of publishers asking for radical rewrites. One of my first ever books was 25,000 words long and had one main protagonist. I was offered publication on condition that I cut the length to 12,000 words and added a second protagonist.

It was daunting for a new author, but also great learning, because I discovered early on in my career that a radical rewrite could be surprisingly easy to do; it could make the story better and actually feel quite exhilarating.

I've just finished the manuscript for *Wildfire*, which will be published next year by A&C Black. They loved the idea for the book but wanted it to run to 5,000 words rather than the 2,000 I suggested, so I needed to extend the plot.

I had a very clear climax to the story, so I wrote the whole plot out backwards, starting from the dramatic ending, and working out all the points where the characters would clash. By the time I had got to the start of the story, I had 20 scenes. I then started from the beginning, writing a detailed plan for each scene with a clear target of the word count needed (so long as the plot could sustain it). It worked really well and I am delighted with the result. I hadn't written backwards before!

Sean Callery

Whether your plot needs sorting out because it doesn't really work or doesn't fit a publisher's requirements, you need to:

- be able to recognise where it doesn't work in its current form

- be willing to chop and change and mess around with your story
- know how to go about it.

Sorting out the structure

The plot is like the skeleton of a book; it has to be strong or the whole thing won't stand up. Just to recap, the backbone of the plot almost always boils down to this: a protagonist wants something, they try to get it, they fail; they try again, they fail; they keep trying, and each time the stakes get higher, until they finally succeed, or accept and reframe their defeat.

The protagonist's problem or goal is what drives the story, and the reader needs to be conscious of it all the way through, because that's what will create, sustain and build tension in the plot.

One of the most common plot problems is when a story lacks this strong central focus. Then the energy gets diffused, the reader's connection with the protagonist is interrupted and a feeling of 'Where is this going?' sets in.

Although I personally hate it when publishers ask for a synopsis before a book is written, because for me a story is an adventure and knowing what happens in advance takes all the fun out of it, at the redraft stage I always write one.

I do it because writing a synopsis is the best possible way to strip your story down to the bones and see what needs changing or moving around.

You aren't trying to charm or intrigue with a synopsis; you're trying to show that you have a convincing and well-constructed plot. There shouldn't be anything woolly about it and no teasers – it's not a blurb.

To find the main thrust of the story, start by distilling it down to three sentences.

The three-sentence synopsis

Write one-sentence answers to each of these questions:

1. What is your protagonist's goal or problem, and why?

For example: Bridget Jones wants to find true love because she doesn't want to be a sad old spinster. There are other things Bridget wants, such as to lose weight and stop drinking so much, but these are not the main issue; they are secondary to her quest for love.

In my Young Adult novel, *Drift*, it's a problem rather than a goal: Jess has stopped talking because she feels overwhelmed and confused by the suicide of her older brother.

2. How do they set about achieving their goal or solving their problem?

For example: Bridget has a relationship with her boss, Daniel Cleaver, and keeps Mark Darcy at arm's length because she believes he has slept with Daniel's fiancée.

In my book: The school counsellor encourages Jess to write to Seb (her brother), which unfreezes her emotions and begins an emotional build-up that eventually results in her shouting at everyone in her English class.

3. What is the outcome for this goal?

For example: Bridget discovers that Daniel has cheated on her and lied about Mark Darcy, and she falls in love with Mark.

Jess is talking normally again and coming to terms with her brother's death.

Once you have got the main thrust of the book very clear in your mind by writing a three-sentence synopsis, write a longer one that lists all the major scenes which directly contribute to the protagonist's achievement of their goal.

This is your major plot line. It shouldn't take up more than about a page of A4. It is what you will send to publishers, to demonstrate that you have made a strong story from your basic idea.

The single-page synopsis

This is not about what your protagonist wants or feels, but what they do. To help you focus on the action, it can help to think about the book as a film, and see what happens in the major scenes.

Start with one sentence to describe the 'inciting incident' – what happens to make your protagonist engage with the challenge of their problem or goal? This sentence isn't the first line of your manuscript, but the action of the first scene.

For example: Bridget Jones meets Mark Darcy at her parents' friends' New Year party, hears him describe her as 'a verbally incontinent spinster' and decides it's time to change her life and find Mr Right.

Then write one sentence for the ending – what happens to resolve it? Again, not the last line but the last piece of action.

For example: Mark buys Bridget a new diary for a new start in her life, and they kiss for the first time.

When you have these two sentences, sketch in the major scenes which move your protagonist from wanting something at the beginning to getting it at the end. Distil it down to one sentence for each scene, and stick to the action; it's about what they do, not how they feel.

For example: Bridget sees Mark again at a book launch but goes for dinner afterwards with Daniel, who tells her Mark slept with his fiancée... Bridget takes Daniel to a family party at a country house hotel and he leaves early... Bridget catches Daniel in his flat with his lover... She leaves her job at the publishing house and gets a new one in TV...

Not all books follow this pattern in such an obvious way, with a string of scenes centred on the protagonist and their struggle, but all stories have to have a main focus, a clear sense of what the issue is at the beginning and a resolution of that issue at the end, then everything in the middle has to move the story forward from A to B.

In *Drift*, for example, the issue of Jess's inability to talk is foregrounded in the very first scene and again at the beginning of each section, when she has another session with the counsellor.

The individual scenes of the story that come out through her letters – the story within a story – don't directly move Jess towards talking, but the build-up of emotion in each section is always pushing her towards it.

When you are satisfied, from writing a single page synopsis, that everything in the story moves the major plot forward from the opening issue to the closing solution, take each scene individually and put it under the microscope.

How far does it contribute to the main plot line? Could it do more if you were to refocus it, build it up or make it shorter? Do you need it at all? This is the time to cut orphan scenes and details that don't lead anywhere.

Is it convincing and plausible? Your readers will certainly spot anything that doesn't ring true or stretches their 'willing suspension of disbelief', so if you have any doubts, don't think you might get away with it.

Supposing your protagonist is a little old lady, like Miss Marple, she can never be involved in a scene which requires her to chase someone, or escape from being chased. Most fictional detectives are mature in years and have a strapping young sergeant to do the chasing.

Every scene must be psychologically plausible, too. Bridget Jones would never have got a job at the BBC because she's too dizzy and disorganised; when she gets an interview with the commercial TV station it's clear the slightly sleazy boss is looking for someone entertaining who he also wouldn't mind sleeping with.

Check that you haven't got several scenes which are similar. Supposing you've got two party scenes, for example, either move the action of one to a different situation, such as a picnic or holiday, or keep it as a party but make it feel really different. *Bridget Jones' Diary*, for example, has several parties in the first half but they're all completely different: a Christmas party at Bridget's parents' home, a launch party in a swanky publishing house, a weekend gathering in a country hotel.

Think of each scene as an episode in a serial. Has it got a cliffhanger ending? Will the reader feel they really have to know what's going to happen next?

Finally, looking at the progression of one scene to another, does the action build in intensity? Supposing your protagonist gets hurt in a fight and decides to carry a knife for protection in future, when he gets in another fight, there will be more serious injuries and more serious consequences. Now he could be a target for revenge, and the next fight he gets into has the potential to be his last.

If the scenes don't build in intensity and you put your protagonist into several situations which have similar consequences – he gets cuts and bruises every time he's in a fight, and he isn't driven to further action - your story might as well sit in front of the TV and convalesce with him.

You may need to pull some earlier scenes back a little if you've gone out too strongly, so that you've got room for the stakes to rise as the story progresses.

But it isn't only in the action that the stakes have to rise; the emotional tension has to keep on building too.

Turning up the emotional temperature

What is the main emotion of your story? If it's a romance, it will be love; if it's a comedy, it will be fun and laughter; if it's a horror story, it may be fear.

Imagine that emotion as a colour. For me, these three examples would be pink, yellow and red. For you, they may be red, green and black. It doesn't matter what colour you imagine the dominant emotion to be, the point is, it needs to grow in intensity.

Bridget Jones' romantic feelings are almost non-existent at the beginning of the story, very pale pink indeed. But they build gradually in both her relationships with Daniel and Darcy; the colour gets richer as the story progresses, and ends in a burst of pure vibrant pink when she and Darcy finally have their first kiss.

In a murder mystery, the detective has to find out who the killer is, and the reader's initial feeling of curiosity as to who did it and why, is mingled with unease at the possibility that the killer could strike again. Unease builds to fear as it becomes clear that someone saw what happened. Fear builds to terror when the killer finds out he was seen and goes after the witness.

You can intensify the emotional arc of your book by also adjusting the shades of black and white. Remember that fiction is not real life. It has to be convincing, but it also has to be exciting. As the French philosopher, Simone Weil said, 'Imaginary evil is romantic and varied; real evil is gloomy, monotonous, barren, boring. Imaginary good is boring; real good is always new, marvellous, intoxicating.'

So see if you can make your protagonist ever more

admirable or likeable, beautiful or vulnerable, and your antagonist even more cruel, selfish, mercenary or loathsome, without turning them into caricatures. Give your protagonist the highest possible motivations and your antagonist the most despicable.

If you can reveal deeper shades of darkness in your antagonist as the plot thickens, your reader's fear for the protagonist will grow more intense, especially if the protagonist is unaware of what his enemy is capable of.

In a romance plot, your hero will already be larger than life, and maybe you could make him even more desirable as the story develops. As the hero grows more wonderful, reveal ever more of his love-rival's darkness. Maybe he has a secret history of violence towards women, or is only pursuing the heroine for her money.

In an adventure story, make the protagonist even more courageous by revealing other great challenges he's had to overcome; maybe he's climbing the mountain because he's terminally ill, so it's even more admirable when he refuses to give up. And maybe the climbing partner he thought was his best friend could be eaten up by secret jealousy and determined to sabotage the expedition.

In a murder mystery, you could make the darkness darker by letting your murderer be a stalker, a sadist or a blackmailer too, and you could make your detective even more admirable by giving her a disabled son or an aged parent to take care of at the same time as she's trying to find the killer, or personal demons such as an alcohol problem or a broken heart.

Sorting out the action and emotional build-up in the major plot line is the main task of the macro-edit. When you have a clear idea of what needs altering or adjusting in the major plot, you can start to consider the secondary characters and subplots.

Sorting out your subplots

Subplots work in the same way as your main plot, but centre on major characters other than your protagonist. What do these characters want? Sketch their plot lines as you did for the main protagonist, starting with a three-sentence synopsis and then a single page one.

The subplots normally start later and are resolved earlier than the main plot, to ensure that the beginning and ending of the story are fully focused on the major plot line.

For example, in Bridget Jones, the first and final scenes are both of Bridget and Mark Darcy. In between, Daniel Cleaver comes along with his own goal – to seduce Bridget.

Subplots have to weave into the main plot line, affecting it and helping to move it along, so in *Bridget Jones' Diary*, everything Daniel says and does affects the development of Bridget's relationship with Mark.

When you have written an outline for one or two secondary characters, insert the scenes that involve them into a copy of your main plot outline.

If any of these scenes don't contribute in some way to the major plot line of the protagonist, consider either adjusting them so that they do, or cutting them.

Create a great beginning and a satisfying ending

However good the plot is, no one will read your book unless the first few pages hook them in, so you need to create a really great beginning. No one will recommend it to their friends if the ending doesn't deliver, so you need a satisfying ending too.

I've bunched them together in this chapter and so should you when you're redrafting, because they are very closely related. A great beginning tells the reader exactly what the issue is, and a satisfying ending delivers the solution.

The beginning of the story is the incident, or 'inciting moment', which sets the protagonist on their quest. For Bridget Jones, it's being at her parents' party in a silly Christmas jumper, hearing Mark Darcy call her a 'verbally incontinent spinster who smokes like a chimney, drinks like a fish and dresses like her mother'; for Jess, in *Drift*, it's her first session with the school counsellor.

The ending is not the same as the climax, but shows the situation after it is resolved. In *Bridget Jones' Diary* it isn't the big dramatic scene when Bridget declares her love for Mark at his parent's anniversary party, but the sweet little scene between Bridget and Mark which shows the situation has changed, and they are finally going out with each other.

In *Drift*, it isn't Jess's dramatic outburst in the English class, but her ordinary family life, where she has got back to talking normally again.

A satisfying ending needs to tie up all the loose ends, with the subplots resolved as well as the main plot. In each case, think about the character's inner life, as well as the events of their story.

What were their thoughts, feelings and motivations at the beginning of the story? How have they changed because of the events of the story? Has each character, especially your protagonist, made a psychological journey?

To take a classical example, at the beginning of *Great Expectations*, by Charles Dickens, Pip is a child of the forge, who loves his guardian, Joe Gargery, and wants to become a blacksmith like him. When his mysterious benefactor pays for his training as a gentleman, he breaks away from his roots altogether and becomes too proud to associate with Joe. But towards the end, when Pip is faced with ruin, it is Joe who bails him out, and he realises his error and expresses his deep shame.

Estella, in that story, begins as Miss Havisham's creature, learning to have no heart; through the middle of the story, she believes she is incapable of loving, but towards the end of the book she finds that she can fall in love.

Thinking about the ending in relation to how it all began means you can often see ways of making small adjustments to the beginning and/or the ending which will tie them together in a subtle but satisfying way.

Faint echoes of the beginning in the ending or the ending in the beginning highlight the circular movement of the story, giving your reader a greater sense of completion.

In *Great Expectations*, the opening scene is young Pip meeting the escaped convict Magwitch on the marshes. It's hugely atmospheric, characterised by mud, mist and dark water, and it's strongly recalled in their final scene together, when they are making their escape in a rowing boat on the muddy waters of the Thames, in the swirling London fog.

Pip's first meeting with Estella is at her childhood home, Satis House, and Dickens brings her back there at the end through the deaths of both her adopted mother, Miss Havisham, and her brutal husband, so that Pip's last meeting with her is once again at Satis House.

This device of echoing the beginning in the ending prompts the reader to reflect back over the whole story and notice the journey the characters have made, both physically and psychologically.

It needn't be big scenes, like in *Great Expectations* – sometimes tweaking a few words will be enough to take your reader back to where it all began and have the sense that this was always where the story was bound to finish.

Look for these echoes in films and books. Notice what makes a beginning that hooks you in, and an ending that feels right and satisfying.

When it comes to redrafting yours, pay particular attention to the opening page.

The first page

The opening page is the most important page in the book because it's where the reader decides whether or not to buy, so take your time over it. Get it right.

With the first draft, you're writing your way in, and you can't tell until you've finished the whole book how much background information your reader really needs early on. Usually they need very little, because they can pick it up as the story progresses, so check your first chapter isn't loaded down with unnecessary back-story.

Sometimes, much more than a few sentences of exposition can be cut, especially if you're writing for adults. Would your story benefit from having the original first few sentences, pages or even chapters simply lopped off? You might well find a cracking opening a little way in to your first draft, because that's often where the real action begins.

Here's the example I give in my children's book, *How to be a Brilliant Writer*.

Start in the middle!

One part of the first draft you can often cut is the beginning. So look at your first few sentences and ask yourself whether the story really needs them. Is there a moment after the beginning that would make a more exciting start?

~~Jazz lived in a terraced house near the railway line with his mum and dad, his sister Isabel and their two cats, Jack and Jester. Sometimes he and his mate, Big Pete, used to go to the bridge to watch the trains. One day, when they were up there waiting,~~ there was a sound like thunder, rumbling along the rails and suddenly the train came whooshing through. In the silence that followed, ~~they~~ *Jazz and Big Pete* saw something lying beside the track. They ran down off the bridge to get a better look.

As well as getting straight into the action, hook your reader in from page one with the sound, style and personality of your story, by making sure that the voice is strong and engaging from the very beginning.

For example, my 'Peony Pinker' books all begin 'You know when...' to set the lively, conversational tone, and friendly personality of the narrator, and go on to describe a specific situation which the reader cannot possibly have experienced, so you know straight away that the book will be funny. Here's the start of *How to Get the Family you Want*, by Peony Pinker:

> You know when your parents are being really annoying such as, for example, when your mum is starting up her own business called 'Garden Angels' and your dad's supposed to be doing more around the house, but isn't?
>
> And they argue all the time until you can't stand another minute of it so you just have to get out of there and take a long walk on the beach with your sister's boyfriend's dog?
>
> Well, that's what happened to me the day that Gran was coming to visit.

Your first page should make it perfectly clear what kind of book this is – funny, historical, political, fantastical, whatever. If you have a main point-of-view protagonist as opposed to the now much more unusual omniscient narrator, it should also express their personality, whether you're writing in the first person or the third.

I'd like to quote you some opening pages from other authors here, but I don't want to spend any more of my life than I already have with *Writing in the House of Dreams* in trying to get permissions.

Anyway, you can read unlimited opening pages now on Amazon, with 'search inside' and I would really recommend that you do. Notice which ones make you personally want to read on and analyse why.

When you hook the reader in straight away with an intriguing set-up and an interesting narrative voice, when you handle the tension skillfully through the middle of your book, your reader will stay with you, knowing they're in good hands, and trust you to deliver a satisfying ending.

One final thing I would say, please resist the temptation to be tricksy. If at any point you tried to create tension in your first draft with teasers such as 'Little did she know...' or 'It was all to go horribly wrong...' root them out.

Don't withhold information either. You know the kind of thing, like when a character unexpectedly leaps to the rescue and then turns out to have been an SAS officer in a former life. You gain an element of surprise but at the cost of belated explanation.

There's no need for tricks if the plot hangs together well. Give the reader all the information they need to be fully in the action as it unfolds. Don't play games with them, teasing forward or holding back. Trust the story and let the reader in.

When it comes to macro-editing non-fiction, you also need to be bold and ruthless. Just as with fiction, you may have to 'kill your darlings', cutting out anything that doesn't directly contribute to your argument or theme, even if you think it's really interesting.

As much as with a novel, the first page of a non-fiction book has to hook the reader in immediately, by getting straight to the point and sparking their interest, and part of what will engage them is the voice.

The importance of voice in non-fiction can be easily overlooked. How many times have you bought a book because the subject sounded interesting only to find that the writing is dull as ditchwater?

Non-fiction can be funny; it can be moving; it can be poetic, or exciting. It can be brisk and economical, or meditative and thoughtful. Non-fiction has a voice, even if you don't want to make your presence as the author felt directly, by using the first person and including your own thoughts and anecdotes.

Most of my non-fiction doesn't come from academic learning; it springs from my own enthusiasms and experiences, and so a personal voice feels appropriate.

If you decide to use a personal voice for your book, think about how you want to come across. Do you want to sound authoritative, approachable, amusing? What would feel most appropriate for the subject matter and approach of your book? What would appeal most to the kind of reader you want to attract?

It can be helpful to put yourself in character when you're checking the voice of your non-fiction, just as you would with fiction. For my adult books on writing, I'm writing as the me who runs my adult workshops, where I try to create an atmosphere that's adventurous yet safe, friendly and encouraging.

But for my children's non-fiction, I write in the character of the child I once was, and the children's writer I am now, so the voice is much lighter and funnier, with loads of jokes and quizzes.

The voice of your book should be clear and strong from the very beginning, and remain consistent until the end.

With non-fiction, it may influence not only the tone but also the content.

For example, if you've decided to go for a serious academic voice you might want to take out the odd personal anecdote that has slipped in at the first draft stage, when you were still undecided. You might want to include more evidence to back up your points instead.

Once the macro-edit is sorted out, you can move from the big picture to the detail; from your material to the way you express it in non-fiction and – in fiction – from the story to the way you tell it.

Summing Up

Redrafting is a process and your book might go through several complete drafts before you feel it's a good as it can be.

When you're putting off redrafting:

- embrace the break – you need to get some distance from the first draft anyway, before you start redrafting
- begin with a full read-through, looking at whether your story has an arresting beginning, a good build-up of tension and a satisfying ending (in non-fiction, an opening that says what the book is about, a clear development of the subject and a conclusion that sums things up)
- at the macro level, be bold
- always, always, always save your previous draft before you make any major changes, and work on a copy.

6 When You're Tempted to Skip Micro-editing

It can be tempting to say 'Okay, that'll do!' once you've wrestled the plot into shape and made a few tweaks to the writing. After all, style problems can always be sorted out with an editor, and therefore, so long as you have a great story, sketchy writing might not be a deal-breaker.

But a story would have to be truly amazing these days for a publisher to want to go that extra mile. One publisher I know drew back from further contracts with an established author because his first few books with them needed so much editing.

And anyway, compared with the macro-edit, the second stage of editing is a walk in the park. You don't need to get an all-encompassing overview with the micro-edit, so there's no need for another complete read-through; you can take the text a section at a time, which means the task doesn't feel too unwieldy.

Focus in on a part of the text/a chapter/page etc rather than trying to redraft half the book. Print off the piece. Choose a coloured pen. Leave your usual workspace and choose a new environment. Now read the piece out loud and focus in on the micro-edit until you are satisfied.

Miriam Halahmy

This is word-level editing, and every word has to be right. You're obviously tidying up any verbal tics such as overuse of 'really' or 'suddenly' or whatever your weakness may be. You're watching out for repetitions such as, in this paragraph, the use of 'such as'.

You're noticing sections where the sentences all have the same length or structure, and introducing more variety of form. For example, you might want to change: 'She went to the shops and bought a newspaper. She got the bus home and put the kettle on. She opened the paper and saw an article about her missing cat...' to something like: 'She bought a newspaper at the shops, went home on the bus and put the kettle on. While she was waiting for it to boil, she opened the paper...' etc.

But the most important task of the micro-edit is to make sure the book has a strong and consistent narrative voice.

Fine-tune the narrative voice

I talked a bit about narrative voice in non-fiction in my chapter on macro-editing because the voice affects the content more in non-fiction and you have to think about voice when you're creating a great beginning.

Now you've got a clear idea of what the voice will be, your micro-edit means going through the whole manuscript with a fine tooth comb, making sure it's consistent.

That's the main job when it comes to fiction too. Most stories these days are written from the protagonist's point of view, whether in the first or third person, so the voice of the book must be their voice, expressive of their outlook and personality, grounded in their social situation and appropriate to their age.

Any inconsistency, even a single word out of character or out of place, can pull your reader back from being swept up in the 'reality' of your story, and remind them that they're reading a book.

For example, if your viewpoint character is a child, any over-complicated words or sentences will immediately cause your reader to suspend disbelief and make child readers feel they're being patronised, because they can see you're a grown-up but you're trying to make them think you're a child.

As well as over-complicated language, you have to avoid anything that is conceptually inappropriate for your child protagonist. For example, if they refer to something that happened before they were born, they will have to explain how they know it. 'Grandpa told me once that there used to be a cornfield where the supermarket is…'

A child will have very limited knowledge of geography and history, politics and sociology too. Your protagonist's experience of the story will be limited by their inexperience of the world.

The things you mention and the responses your protagonist has to them must also be appropriate to the interests of a child. Generally speaking, older children are not particularly interested in the adults around them; they're much more interested in their peers.

Mum could be trying to get pregnant again, Dad could be about to make the presentation of his career, but the really interesting thing is Fred next door's work-in-progress water slide, or best friend Jem's new pony. Adult concerns may be in the mix, but only insofar as they directly affect your protagonist's day-to-day life, and they'll almost always be in the background.

Supposing your viewpoint character is an old crofter who has never been anywhere bigger than their local market town. If your story takes them to London, they're going to be filled with wonder, horror, excitement; they'll notice the smell of the kebab shop or the tatty pigeons on the pavement, all the things a city dweller is unlikely to remark on.

Your old crofter may be preoccupied with trying to understand the ticket system for the London buses; they may feel anxious about going down into the Underground. The way they write about the experience of going to London will be completely different from the way someone who commutes in from Basingstoke every day might describe it.

It's a good idea, before you begin your micro-edit, to have another look at your notes for the point-of-view character. Get under their skin again, get into their head, using the techniques I described in Chapter 3.

If you come back to your story thinking and feeling like your point-of-view character, you will automatically recognise when the voice is wrong. You will see where the book describes something in a way 'you' wouldn't describe it, or focuses on something 'you' aren't interested in.

For example, I was editing a story recently with a ten-year-old protagonist, written in the third person. Several times in the text, the author referred to his size, in sentences like 'He squeezed his little body through the opening of the tunnel.' and 'He ran as fast as his little legs could carry him.'

Even though this is written in the third person 'he', rather than the first person 'I', the whole story is supposed to be seen through his eyes, and a child would not think of himself as small, only an adult would.

When you read through your story in character, you will bring your character's personality to it, so if you're an artist or fashion designer, you'll give us colours, shapes and styles in everything you see; you'll show us your story through an artist's eyes.

If you're a counsellor, you'll be most interested in the inner lives of the people around you, so you'll notice their body language and conversational styles, but you might not notice details in the physical environment at all.

There is usually lots of opportunity to sharpen up the voice at the redrafting stage because you hardly knew the protagonist when you started writing the first draft, whereas by the end of it you've come to know them really well.

As well as the narrative voice, you will want to make sure the style and tone of the book is consistent and strong. If it's a funny story, could you make it funnier? If it's a scary story, could you make it scarier?

Think about the literary register you're going for too. If it's a genre novel, you will want to edit with the conventions of your genre in mind. If it's a literary novel, the language will need to be rich and varied, and never clichéd.

An excellent way of focusing your mind on what kind or story it is, the literary register and the narrative voice, is by writing a blurb. Take a moment to read the backs of some books that are similar to yours and get the feel for what a blurb should be.

Writing a blurb

A blurb is not the same as a synopsis; it doesn't give away the story. A blurb is a taster and a teaser, designed to give the reader a flavour of what's inside.

The blurb should be written in the style, tone and register of the book, to appeal to your target reader. Is there lots of dialogue in your book? Include some in your blurb.

Is it genre fiction with clichéd characters? Go for it!

'Handsome billionaire businessman, Mark Blaydon, wants to develop a golf course on Hamperdown Fields. Shy schoolteacher, Sherrilee James, is determined to stop him…'

If the book is written in the first person, you could write the blurb in the first person too, or third person but through the eyes of the protagonist.

'Gina's been expelled from school, but Mrs Bryson's always had it in for her…'

'Yeah, so I got thrown out of school, big deal. Baggy Bryson's always had it in for me…'

Experiment with it, and try to distil it down into one or two short paragraphs that express:

1. The situation
2. The problem
3. The hopeful possibility
4. The mood.

Here's one of mine, from *How to Get the Family You Want*, *by Peony Pinker*, which starts straight in with the protagonist, her situation (fed up with her family), the various problems she's got with them all, and the hope that she might be able to cope with it. The tone is humorous and conversational, and expresses both the mood and personality of the protagonist.

Peony Pinker is sick of

- Mum and Dad (arguing non stop)
- big sister Primrose (total drama queen)
- nobody listening (as usual)
- Dennis the rabbit (the man promised he was house-trained…)

Gran says you can't change your family. Can Peony learn to live with them instead?

Finally, remember that the title and chapter headings are also part of the style and voice of the book. Is your working title still a good fit? Now that you know the whole book inside and out, could you come up with a better one? Make a shortlist and ask your friends and fellow writers which one would be most likely to make them want to read the book.

Write a table of contents, so you can see more clearly whether the chapter headings, if you have any, are doing as much as they might.

Each of my 'Peony Pinker' books has seventeen chapters, which all have two-part titles such as: 'Beans for Tea and

World War Three', 'One Week's Trial and Two Kinds of Poos' and 'The Dead of the Night and Dennis's Disappearing Whiskers'.

Writing in the House of Dreams has four parts, with titles that extend the metaphor in the book's title: 'Crossing the Threshold', 'The House of Dreams', 'The Landscape Beyond' and 'Into the Dream-space.'

Each part has three chapters, with titles such as: 'The Call to Dreams', 'The Beast in the Basement', 'Where Dreamers Meet' and 'The Cloths of Heaven'. You can feel how all the titles give a flavour of the book.

Creating a strong cohesive voice and style is the most important part of your micro-edit for both fiction and non-fiction, but there are other tools in the writer's toolbox that can help you give your book extra sparkle and shine.

Use all the tools in your toolbox

The magical thing about writing fiction is that we are able to transfer what we see in our own imagination into the reader's imagination, and one way we do that is through describing what we're seeing.

But there has to be just the right amount of description. Too much, and the story can get bogged down; too little, and your reader may struggle to engage.

Description and details

I tend to write lean because I'm impatient to find out how the action is going to work, so I always have to add description and detail at the editing stage. You might also skimp on description if you haven't imagined the scene fully enough in the first place.

Take your time re-imagining each scene. The way to make your settings come alive for yourself is through the senses. Describing what your protagonist is seeing, hearing, tasting, feeling and smelling is one way to make them come alive for your reader, because then they can see, hear, taste, feel and smell it too.

But your reader doesn't want pages and pages of description, just the telling detail, and if you've fully imagined the scene you will instinctively know which details to give. A word can indicate the season or weather; a short sentence, the sound of traffic or the scent of orange blossom.

Sometimes you can give much more information without actually adding any extra words at all, by simply swapping a general noun for a more specific one. For example, supposing your protagonist can hear birds outside the window – what kind of birds?

If you swapped the word 'birds' for 'skylarks' your reader would automatically picture a summer day, and an open surrounding landscape. Seagulls, chickens, sparrows, robins, woodpeckers... each one would conjure, in one single word, a completely different setting.

Suppose your protagonist buys yellow flowers for her friend – roses or daffodils? One tells the reader it's springtime, the other could be any time of year these days but is still most suggestive of summer. If they're freesias, many readers would also automatically imagine their wonderful smell.

Does the action take place in a seaside town? Name it. Eastbourne says something quite different from Newquay. Has your protagonist got new dinner plates? Wedgewood suggests a whole domestic setting that is not Ikea.

Does your protagonist drive a small car? Tell us it's a Ford Fiesta – then we can picture it exactly. Does she have a big dog? A Labradoodle tells us something about her that isn't at all the same as we might get from a German Shepherd.

You only have to give these details once because after that the reader has the image planted in their mind and that's what they'll see every time the protagonist gets in her car or takes her dog for a walk.

Everything carries connotations and cultural assumptions, so be aware that every detail can be telling. Even the names you give your characters carry information for the reader.

Age, class, geography, even personality can be suggested in a name. How old is Margaret Sweet? What's her job, where's she from, what's she like? How about Roly Smythe, Rick Wilde, Chardonnay Wilkins, Sky MacIntyre?

When I do this in a group, asking everyone to jot down a brief description of a character just from a name, it's amazing how many of them come up with the same things, even down to the character's specific job or personality.

In passing, on the subject of names, try not to have several characters whose names sound similar or start with the same letter, because this will make it much easier for your reader to remember who is who.

Refining the details is a way of not only adding layers of unspoken description but also cutting the length of the text, which is win-win for the pace and effectiveness of your story.

Another way of cutting words but adding effect is by using more powerful verbs so that you don't need to weigh things down with adverbs. When it comes to adjectives and adverbs, less is more, even though you obviously can't cut them out altogether.

For example, instead of the non-specific verb plus adverb combination in 'she went restlessly around the house' you could use a single more powerful verb, 'she moped around the house'; instead of 'he waited impatiently at the bus-stop', you could say 'he couldn't wait to get home'.

Show-don't-tell

Powerful verbs can be part of 'show, don't tell'. When you're redrafting, notice when you're telling the reader how a character feels and see if you can show how he feels in his actions instead. This is more dynamic and also enables you to cut more adjectives and adverbs.

Supposing your first draft says: 'Jack felt annoyed. He left the room angrily.' This tells the reader how the character is feeling with an adjective ('annoyed') and an adverb 'angrily'.

You could show what the character is feeling instead, by replacing the adjective and adverb with two powerful verbs – 'Jack bristled. He stormed out of the room.'

Another common way of telling-not-showing is the use of abstract nouns. You can replace them with powerful verbs as well. 'When she saw his face, Deirdre was full of sadness/fear/love' sounds far less dynamic than, 'When she saw his face, Deirdre sighed/ trembled/ melted'.

We feel emotion in the body and if, instead of saying

'he felt' or 'she felt' you describe the bodily sensation of his grief or her tenderness, you reader will feel it in their own body, and connect on a visceral level.

'Emily was scared. She stepped gingerly onto the diving board' tells us how she's feeling; 'Emily's heart was pounding as she stepped onto the diving board' makes us feel it ourselves.

'Show, don't tell' is all about changing unnecessary description into action. Actions speak louder than words, and you don't need to tell us your protagonist is well-mannered and considerate if that's the way we see him behaving in the story.

All the information your reader needs to know about your characters should be clear from the way they behave, including the way they speak to others.

Dialogue

This brings me on to dialogue, which is another area to think about when you're redrafting. Dialogue adds variety to the text but it should never be just an add-on. Real-life conversations are often random and inconsequential but you aren't transcribing real life.

In fiction, every piece of dialogue should fulfil a function in the story, either conveying information or moving the action on.

The way your characters talk tells the reader a lot about them in terms of their age and social situation, their regional roots and personality. The things they say show their attitudes towards other characters, and demonstrate the relationship between them.

Dialogue can also provide an opportunity for filling in background plot information in a natural and unobtrusive way because it means you can avoid awkward-sounding pluperfect passages such as, 'Helena had heard that Jeremy had had a relationship with her best friend, Jude, a few years previously, when they had both been working at the Foreign Office.'

'Didn't you go out with Jude a few years ago?' Helena asked.

'Yes, when we were both at the Foreign Office.'

Job done!

As well as using it to fill in the background, dialogue can move the plot forward in a pacy and economical way. There's nothing wrong with saying: 'They didn't want to stay at the hotel because it was shabby and not very clean so they decided to try and find a better one.' However, it would be more punchy as dialogue: '"Let's find somewhere else," said Harry. "This place is a dump."'

Putting it in dialogue, as well as moving the action on more economically, has the added value of expressing the personality of Harry.

To make your dialogue feel natural, stick to 'said' – it's unobtrusive and the reader barely notices it. This is one area where you aren't trying to avoid repetition. You don't have to indicate who's speaking every single time because quite often it's obvious from the back-and-forth of the conversation.

Use 'asked' or 'replied' sparingly – 'said' is fine in question-and-answer conversations too. Use variations which carry extra information such as 'yelled' or 'whispered' even more sparingly, and avoid fancy alternatives such as 'opined' or 'remonstrated' altogether.

When you're writing dialogue, think of it as a scene. What are the characters doing while they're having this conversation? Where are they? One way of making it feel more natural is to include little snippets of description or action in among the things they say.

"'What time do you call this?" Mr Jensen said, tapping his watch with his finger.

Ellen struggled out of her coat and grabbed her uniform.

"Sorry, Mr Jensen. I couldn't get away...'"

Imagery

Finally, when you're doing your micro-edit, think about your use of imagery. Images are pictures, and a picture paints a thousand words, so they can be a brilliant way of enriching your writing.

For example, Reggie Perrin always pictured his mother-in-law as a hippo, which says a lot about her and also about him. In my story, *How to get what you want, by Peony Pinker*, Peony imagines each member of her family as a dog. Her attention-seeking sister is a Pekingese, her mum's a lively sheepdog and her dad's a comfortable old Labrador.

Original images are more effective than ones that have become commonplace, or even clichéd, such as 'a sandwich short of a picnic', 'like a bull in a china shop' or 'as pretty as a picture', so consider creating your own.

For my *Car-mad Jack* books I used images for comic effect by suggesting incongruous juxtapositions. Jack was 'as happy as a fish in a sandpit' when he knew his big cousin was going to visit, because his cousin was 'as nice as poison pie'.

Obviously, any images you use have to be appropriate for the style and subject of your book. They may be poetic and lyrical, exciting and exotic. They may be one-off embellishments, or repeated like a refrain, such as Reggie's hippo every time he thinks about his mother-in-law.

Sometimes an image can describe the whole subject of the book, to the extent that you might even use it in your title. Some that spring to mind would be *To Kill a Mockingbird*, *Heart of Darkness*, *The Hippopotamus*, and *The Lion and the Rose*.

I used an image for the title of my non-fiction book *Writing in the House of Dreams*, but the tools in your toolbox for non-fiction are generally not the same as the ones you use with fiction.

Instead of description, show-don't-tell and dialogue, with non-fiction you've got a whole range of special features.

The special features of non-fiction

Where fiction is almost invariably laid out as plain text, non-fiction may be organised in a variety of different ways. Chapters can be split into sections with sub-headings and sub-sub-headings; paragraphs can be rendered more economically by bullets and numbered lists.

Information can be conveyed effectively through the use of visual elements such as charts, diagrams, graphs, maps and illustrations, which may offer you the opportunity of reducing or even replacing some passages of text.

With some kinds of non-fiction, you can use quizzes and questionnaires to get your point across in a more interactive way.

Then there are boxes, which mean you can include things that sit outside the main narrative, such as exercises, tips, quotations, anecdotes and interesting facts.

Non-fiction can look more varied and exciting than fiction on the page, but we often forget that when we're working on the first draft because we're just trying to organise our ideas.

At the micro-redraft stage, think about how you could use the special features of non-fiction to make your book more easy, accessible and enjoyable to read than continuous text.

Finally, don't forget the back-matter. Non-fiction often includes notes and references, indexes, bibliographies and other useful information, but this isn't a one-size-fits-all. What you decide to add at the end of your book will depend about its voice and nature.

For example, because this book feels personal, from me to you, I've added a list of the websites and organisations I've mentioned in the text and can personally recommend, rather than a selection that I've researched online. My bibliography is a list of my own favourite books on writing.

When you have finished redrafting on both the structural and the language level, rest your manuscript again. Then after a few days or weeks, read through the whole thing once more, only this time read it aloud.

If you can find a willing audience, read some of it to other people too. Having a listener can make you even more aware of any gaps that need filling, slow bits that need cutting or passages which simply don't flow very well.

I've been teaching adults for years now and they consistently say that the most useful editing tip I give them is to read their work aloud, however silly they feel! If they can read to an audience, even better – that really shows up the flaws! Several of my students come to my classes principally so they can read their work aloud, I think, as we always include an opportunity to do that for those who want to. I certainly find it true myself – or I wouldn't tell them to do it!

Meg Harper

If you're lucky, you'll know when the book is completely finished because you'll have that punching the air feeling. More often, you'll decide it's time to stop even though there are still imperfections because otherwise you could keep tinkering with it forever.

Knowing your book, for all that it isn't perfect, is the best you can make it is a very good feeling too, much better than sending off or self-publishing a patchy book and hoping that readers will love it anyway.

Every writer is different. I know some who really struggle with the first draft and it's only the thought of having something they can work on at the end of it that keeps them going.

If, like me, you prefer the first draft and would much rather go on and start a new project than go back and do redrafting, the answer might be to read about the craft of writing, so that you'll feel more confident and keen to try out new techniques.

Summing Up

On the micro level, go through the whole text a section at a time, checking that:

- you have a strong, consistent narrative voice
- you have made best use of description, dialogue and imagery, and tried to 'show and not tell'
- you have made the best possible use of the special features of non-fiction if your book is factual

At least once during the process, read through the whole book out loud.

7 When You're Pondering Publication

Publication used to be an unrealisable dream for many writers but now, with the advent of indie publishing, it has become a real possibility for every writer and every book.

This means the first thing you have to decide, when you have finished your book, is whether or not you actually want it to be published. We tend to assume that the only point in writing is to publish and make money, but I've met many writers who don't feel that way, or at least not about every piece of work.

For me, the things I write for publication are my bread and butter writing; I do a lot of playing around with ideas alongside that, just for my own amusement and pleasure. I've also written several memoirs simply as a way of experimenting with different versions of my past, without ever having the least intention of publishing them.

Writing is becoming a popular tool for self-development and problem-solving, and one of the organisations I belong to, Lapidus (strapline: 'Words for Wellbeing'), provides workshops designed to give people the experience of writing as a source of inspiration and understanding.

Besides the projects we write for ourselves, there may be others we only want to share with family, groups of friends or organisations we belong to, producing a small number of personal copies rather than releasing them to the world.

If you have written your book intending for it to be published, you still have to bear in mind, once it is finished, that it might not actually be fit for publication.

Some ideas simply don't work out as well as you expected them to; some can turn out to have been too ambitious for your current writing abilities. If you are new to writing, or this particular book is a new kind of writing for you, then it might be more like a practice piece, helping you to develop the skills you need in order to write another one that will be publishable.

If you suspect that your book isn't good enough, don't try to convince yourself that no one will notice its weaknesses and flaws, or that some people might love it in spite of them. Accept that, at the very least, it will need some work before you go for publication, and if the idea isn't strong enough it may never be publishable at all.

Don't waste agents' and publishers' time by sending them half-baked manuscripts because you'll only be wasting your own time too, and don't self-publish books that aren't up to standard, especially if you are thinking about writing as a career. A book that's garlanded with one-star reviews will definitely not help you to sell your next title, or develop your reputation as an author.

So how can you tell whether your book is good enough? Find some readers you can trust to give you honest and objective feedback, listen to what they say and be willing to go back to the drawing board if you think their suggestions could help you to make your manuscript better.

If you've never been published before, you could send your work to a reading agency such as Cornerstones for a detailed professional assessment.

Quality control is important, not just because you want to build a strong brand as an author, but also because, if you feel confident in the quality of your book, it will be much easier to champion and promote it.

Feeling confident in the quality of your book will also help you to cope with any negative reviews you get or, nearly as bad, getting no reviews at all. Many good books, both indie and traditionally published, sink without trace, never finding readers or making money, so your belief in yourself and your book must be able to withstand a battering.

When you are sure you want to get your book published, you need to decide whether to take the traditional route or go it alone. Most people still assume the traditional route is always best for every book and every author, but the publishing world is changing.

Traditional publishing is wonderful for some books and some authors, but not for all. Now that indie publishing has become more respectable and mainstream its advantages are making it look like a viable alternative.

The traditional route is still the first choice

It is famously difficult to secure a contract with a publisher but there are huge benefits if you can, so I would say that if you decide you want your book to be published, it's definitely worth trying.

If you can place your book with a major publisher, you will get:

- upfront payment, either a flat fee or an advance on royalties
- a far greater likelihood of foreign and film deals, with your agent or publisher handling the rights
- an editor who loves and champions your book, which is wonderfully affirming
- the best possible production for your book, with editing, design, printing and marketing all done by top professionals
- access to professional bodies and eligibility for major prizes, although these opportunities are gradually opening up for self-published authors too
- kudos, because being traditionally published establishes your credentials as an author
- a big boost to your confidence, both in yourself as an author and in your book.

So how do you go about it?

How to find a traditional publisher

You can approach publishing houses directly but your manuscript is much more likely to be read if it's submitted by an agent. This is partly because agents are the initial gatekeepers; they only take on a tiny proportion of the authors who send work to them, so publishers know that anything they submit is likely to be worth looking at.

Agents will also usually offer editorial advice and support to their clients to help them bring a promising manuscript up to publishable standard, so publishers know that every book which comes through an agent is going to be good quality.

You can find details of literary agents in your country online, along with advice on how to apply to them, and many UK authors use the invaluable *Writers' & Artists' Yearbook*. Don't take it personally if agents reject you – many probably will, before you find the one.

Trying to find an agent is often the first lesson in developing the thick skin and cast-iron self-belief you will need if you want to be a published author. I will never forget one of my early rejection letters from an agent, which said: 'I regret to inform you that this agency only represents authors who either can write or else have something interesting to say.' Ouch!

Don't be crushed, but do take note if several agents reject you for the same reasons. Most agents are lovely people with a passion for books and authors, not rude egomaniacs like the one who put me down when I was just starting out, and there can be useful information in rejections.

Although it can be very hard to find an agent to take you on, I think it's pretty much essential if you want to be traditionally published, and there are lots of other benefits as well.

Your agent will be someone who believes in you and your writing, someone who can give you professional feedback and advice. He or she will be a bridge between you and the publishing world, which can feel mysterious, remote and hard to understand, especially in the early days.

In the course of your career, you may work with different publishers, but your agent will always be there. They will be someone you can trust; they may well come to feel like a friend.

Agents normally take 15% of the money an author earns

from their writing. It sounds like a lot, but it is good value. As well as being your champion and your ticket into the traditional publishing world, your agent will take care of all the financial complications that come with publication.

They will negotiate the best possible deal for you with publishers, check royalty statements, chase up payments, look after your foreign and subsidiary rights, and explain things to you when you don't understand the ins and outs of it all.

Some agencies also offer their clients extras such as writing workshops, media training and support with self-publishing for books that have either not found a publisher or gone out of print.

Finally, an agent can reassure you if the reality of being published by a major publisher doesn't fit with the dream. In the first year I was published, my agent placed six books for me, with five different publishers, but all the advances were so low I couldn't imagine how anyone could make a living as an author. She helped me get over my initial disappointment and take a longer view.

My experience was not exceptional.

The hard financial facts

The traditionally published author has no upfront costs because the publisher pays for editing, design, production and distribution. They also pay the author an advance on royalties, which can buy him or her time to work on the next project.

But traditional publishing is big business, and it has changed to reflect changes in society.

In traditional publishing now, we're seeing a growing gap between the small percentage of authors who receive huge advances and all the rest, who don't. The rich are getting richer and the poor are getting poorer.

A lot of new authors are surprised and disappointed by their first advance, and most established authors have seen their advances shrinking over recent years.

Experience and a proven track record don't guarantee security and income. In fact respectable sales and a dedicated following, which once would have been the foundation for a long career, can actually be a disadvantage in the current market, because if you've enjoyed moderate sales for a long time, publishers might decide you've reached your level, and drop you in favour of a new writer who seems to have more bestseller potential.

Should you be that new writer, who gets a big advance for your first two books, you may still not be home and dry. Your publisher, wanting to recoup their investment, will spend a large part of their marketing budget on you and your book, but if sales are disappointing even in spite of that, your fledgling career could end up dead in the water.

With marketing and publicity, as with advances, the gap between the chosen few and the rest is very wide. Publishers will lay on lavish launch parties and organise big book tours and events for the few, while the less-favoured majority will be lucky to get a batch of promotional bookmarks.

In a crowded market, with no marketing spend and deep discounting, a book is unlikely to do more than earn out the advance, which will have been estimated according to how much the publisher thinks you are likely to earn in royalties over the lifetime of the book.

The man in the street would struggle to believe how low most authors' advances are. A couple of thousand pounds is normal, or even a couple of hundred, and some publishers offer royalties only deals, with no advance payment at all.

Where an advance is agreed, it will often be split into three payments, with the author receiving a third on signing the contract, a third on delivering the manuscript and a third on publication.

Sometimes the advance may be split into two payments instead of three, one on signing and one on publication, which is even worse for the author because instead of receiving two thirds before the long wait for publication, he or she will have received only half.

This may be negotiable by the time you've got a publisher interested enough in your book to make an offer, and ideally you'd be looking for the advance to be half on signature and half on delivery of the manuscript, or an uneven three way split with only a token amount held back until publication.

Once the book is published, authors don't start earning royalties until the advance is earned out, and this can take a very long time because the royalty share is often much smaller than the traditional 7.5% on paperbacks and 10% on hardbacks.

Children's authors have always tended to receive a lower royalty rate – I get 5-6% on most of my paperbacks – and they may be expected to share even that with the illustrator these days, especially if the illustrator has a higher profile.

These percentages represent the most an author can

earn; they don't apply to all sales. Where publishers agree deep discount rates with retailers, the author's percentage also drops.

Some publishers pay royalties on net receipts which, with major retailers demanding discounts of up to 80%, means the author's share can end up being virtually nothing.

Of course, there is always the chance that your book will sell much better than expected, or go on selling for longer, and you'll continue receiving payments for years after the advance has earned out, even on such a paltry percentage; that possibility is what keeps most authors going.

However, in some areas of the market the royalties option is not even offered. Some non-fiction and virtually all educational books are now negotiated on a flat-fee basis, which feels very unfair.

The 'industry standard' royalty rate for eBooks, which is 25%, also feels unfair but, so far, traditional publishers have refused to budge on it, even though their actual costs, with no warehousing and distribution, are very low.

The financial arrangements between authors and publishers are becoming even more complicated with the advent of ebooks and print-on-demand paperbacks. Because these need never go out of print, authors would never be able to claim their rights back even if the publisher was selling a couple of copies a year, so it's a question of agreeing a licensing term.

You can find full, clear, up-to-date information and guidelines on publishing contracts on the Society of Authors website, along with all manner of other useful information.

Besides the pressure on royalty payments, another source

of dissatisfaction for authors is twice-yearly accounting, which used to make sense when everything had to be done by snail mail and cheques, but is completely unnecessary in this digital age.

In terms of other income besides royalties, most UK authors will be entitled to regular payments from Public Lending Right for library loans, but the figures are still very small. Of the 22,372 registered authors in the last distribution, over 16,000 received payments of under £100 and 3,400 received between £100 and £500. The maximum payment for any author is £6,600, but only 297 authors were paid over £5,000.

Some authors, especially in the field of education, also receive payments from the Authors' Licensing and Collecting Society for things like photocopying of their copyrighted works, but even that small source of income was under threat recently when the UK government tried to exempt itself from having to pay for copying material within the education system.

Taking into account all income from books, recent research by the Authors' Licensing and Collecting Society in the UK found that only 11% of professional authors (those who dedicate the majority of their time to writing) earn their whole living from writing, and the typical income of a professional author is £11,000 a year, less than two thirds of the Joseph Rowntree Foundation's Minimum Income Standard earnings.

Most people who earn their living from writing do not manage it on the strength of their income from books, but from a range of activities that are made possible because they are published.

For example, many children's authors earn the bulk of their income from doing school visits, although these are getting harder to come by with cuts to school budgets.

Others supplement their income by doing talks and appearances but, as with school visits, a surprising number of organisers seem to expect authors to be willing to work for nothing, cover their own expenses and even feel grateful for the chance to meet potential readers and hand-sell some books.

Many literary festivals pay authors a nominal fee or nothing at all for doing sessions that people have paid good money to attend. Is that fair? I don't think so. It makes me cross.

The Society of Authors publishes guidelines for what you should charge for events and appearances and I personally think that, in the interests of solidarity with other authors, no one should offer freebies unless in exceptional circumstances.

For example, I once did a series of workshops at my local primary school for nothing because I wanted the chance to try out some of the ideas I use in adults' workshops with children, and make sure they worked before I started charging for them.

Many authors, like me, top up their income through teaching creative writing to adults or children, either privately or within the system. Some offer one-to-one mentoring or manuscript appraisal.

There are fixed-term opportunities such as residencies and the Royal Literary Fund fellowship scheme. Grants and prizes may help some authors make ends meet.

Being traditionally published very rarely means a writer

can instantly give up the day job; it's more often the first building block in a portfolio career of writing-related activities, and the writer's capacity to earn may be in relation to their willingness to accept creative compromise.

Some creative constraints

As well as financial pressure the traditionally published author can face increasing pressure on their creative freedom. Contracts may include a 'non compete' clause, under which an author can't publish anything without the permission of their publisher. If enforced, this would mean effectively giving up creative control of your career.

Supposing you want to write more than the one or two books a year your publisher can include on their list? Or supposing – as has happened to some of my writing friends – your publisher keeps delaying a decision for months or years on a manuscript they don't want to take on but equally don't want someone else to publish?

This clause is often waived because most publishers can see the benefits in allowing you to find publishers for books they don't want to take on and self-publish others in order to build your reputation and readership, as that will most probably help sales of the books you've published with them.

But the fact remains that non-compete clauses mean you are asked to give up your legal right to make your own career decisions. You are also likely to be asked to agree to give your publisher first refusal rights for your next book, and you should read the terms and conditions very carefully before agreeing to that.

You may also face pressure to change your work in such a way as to make it more suitable for the mass market.

> It's not difficult to find yourself losing your way and writing something that's not true to who you are. I've done it. I've written more sex into a book to please an agent. I've written crime fiction, invented a serial killer, ditched one book and moved onto the next, and more. . . Being new to writing I was vulnerable to such persuasions (which I have no doubt at all were made from a genuine desire to help me get a book deal). I wouldn't do it like that a second time round because in the end if you're not writing from your own truth the writing is not truly yours.
>
> Costa award-winning Indie author Avril Joy, *From Writing With Love*.

In children's writing, a lot of new and established authors can only get into the market or keep being published by writing series fiction such as 'Rainbow Magic' and 'Beast Quest', where authors work from plots devised in-house by a team of editors.

With mass-market series fiction, authors don't only give up creative control but even their right to be named as the author. A similar trend is ghost-writing for celebrities, where the author's work is published under the name of a famous footballer, say, or ballerina, who will incidentally earn a lot more by simply giving their name to the project than the author does for doing all the writing.

Marketability is the name of the game. Celebrity names and long-running series produced to a formula by many authors under one brand name such as 'Daisy Meadows' are obvious ways to achieve bulk sales.

Original work submitted to the big five traditional publishers has to do more than win over the commissioning editor; it has to win over the marketing department, and their values are not the same.

A few years ago, I proposed an idea for a children's series to an editor I'd worked with before, and she loved it. Bursting with enthusiasm, she asked for four story outlines, then another two, to take to the acquisitions meeting. Although I was slightly reticent about making that kind of commitment, I couldn't help feeling excited.

In the end, the series didn't get a contract with that publisher because my editor couldn't get the marketing department on board with it. When she told me how disappointed she felt, I realised that this situation must be tough for editors as well as authors.

Your book will succeed or fail depending upon how well the marketing people think the concept and title will sell. They usually will not even have read the book, so a yes or no from them doesn't reflect the quality of your writing, but just how easily it will fit into the market.

My series did find another publisher, but other books I've written have failed because they have been deemed 'too niche'. *Writing in the House of Dreams*, for example, received overwhelmingly positive feedback from editors, but no contract.

'An inspirational idea' said one editor; 'a rich feast that sets off all sorts of sparks and recognitions in the reader' said another; 'very readable indeed' said a third, 'I read it in one sitting.'

But then: 'with such a niche topic, we'd struggle to get a good number of copies into shops'; 'the sales would be too modest'; 'a company the size of ours can't make enough of a go of books on this subject as they would need to'.

Two of these big publishers suggested to my agent that a small independent might be able to make a go of my book, as they don't need to make such big sales. If your book is too niche for the mainstream, you might consider that too. The advance and publicity budget will be much smaller, but they will usually dedicate more time and energy to every book they take on, because they take very few.

Writing in the House of Dreams did not find a traditional publisher, but the feedback from editors affirmed for me that it was of publishable quality and, in a way, I felt relieved. I had enough experience to know that even if you can secure a deal, your book may not have a smooth ride going down the traditional route.

My worst-case scenario was that the book might secure a contract with a traditional publisher, take the usual twelve to eighteen months to reach publication, make only modest sales and quickly go out of print. Then there would be more delays while I retrieved the rights before I could publish it myself.

The normal shelf life of a traditionally published book is much shorter than it used to be, with books often going out of print after one print run of a couple of thousand copies. It's not unheard-of for a series to go out of print before the last few commissioned books are even published, if the first have failed to reach their expected sales.

Or, another worst-case scenario, after being taken on

my book might never actually reach publication. I know someone whose book was placed with a major publisher on the strength of the biggest national book chain agreeing to sell it; when they changed their mind and pulled out, so did the publisher. More heartbreak; more delays.

There can be significant benefits in being traditionally published, but the way it is now, with huge advances and publicity spend for the few and decreasing investment in the many, with low royalties and infrequent payments, high sales targets and creative constraints, it doesn't always feel author-friendly.

It's hard to break into traditional publishing and hold your place; to earn your living and feel happy there. Even successful authors are beginning to look upon self-publishing as an attractive alternative or at least a viable second string to their bow.

Self-publishing has advantages too

Only a few years ago, self-publishing was generally looked down upon. Like vanity publishing in the pre-digital age, it was seen as the last resort for writers who had failed to make the grade.

But all that has changed, and it's largely to do with sales. Self-published books now make up a sizeable proportion of the total book market, and individual authors can earn a lot of money and reach a lot of readers through their self-published titles. Most don't, of course, but then again, neither do a lot of traditionally published authors.

Another reason why self-publishing is working is that, with mainstream publishing so driven by bulk sales and the next bestseller, the most exciting creative developments are happening on the margins. As well as unusual and remarkable books, whole new genres such as fan fiction are coming from self-published authors.

There are stands and presentations for self-published authors at major book fairs, and self-published authors with healthy sales may be invited to appear at festivals. Increasingly, indie authors are setting up their own professional events, such as the virtual conference, IndieReCon, timed to coincide with the London Book Fair.

Where membership of authors' societies used to be strictly for those who were traditionally published, now a self-published author can be accepted on the strength of their sales figures.

There are also new professional associations specifically for self-published authors, such as the Alliance of Independent Authors, set up by the formidable Orna Ross.

As the world of publishing grows bigger, so do the ways into it and, for beginners, self-publishing can be a way of showcasing your work, attracting the attention of agents and publishers, and learning about the industry.

It is also becoming a positive choice for established midlist authors, who already have confidence in their writing, experience of doing publicity and an established profile, but are currently getting the worst deal in traditional publishing.

I thought long and hard before I decided to self-publish *There Must Be Horses* instead of submitting it to publishers. Factors that entered into that decision were:

- I thought it would be fun (which it is)
- I wanted to be in control so no one could tell me to change the main character's name or insist the cover should be pink
- I didn't want to sign a traditional publishing contract with a non-competing works clause
- I wanted to earn more per copy than I was receiving on books sold at high discount.

Over a year later, I have no regrets. I'm glad I self-published and I will definitely do so again. I may not have sold as many copies as I would have done if I'd published the traditional way, but the book has already covered all its development costs so every penny it earns now is profit. And those pennies add up quickly because I get 70% of sale price from Kindle Direct Publishing instead of 25% of price received on eBooks sales with a traditional publisher.

Diana Kimpton

Self-publishing can offer the author greater creative freedom and financial control but it does involve a lot of work, time and learning if you do everything yourself – or a lot of cash if you hire other people to do it for you.

The first job is to decide how you want to go about it.

Self-publishing options

When it comes to self-publishing, you can decide how much you want to do yourself – from almost everything to very little. You can do your own jacket design and formatting, and submit your files to different selling platforms yourself; you can employ a team of people to do those jobs and become the project manager, or you can hand the whole thing over to a publishing service.

Your decision about how to go about it will probably be influenced by how much time you've got and how much you're prepared to spend. The best advice I've heard is: don't spend more than you can afford to lose.

If you do everything yourself, it can cost virtually nothing to produce an eBook or even a paperback, now that we have the technology for print-on-demand. You no longer need to buy in bulk to get a good deal on short print runs with independent printers; you can sell paperback versions of your books through companies such as Amazon's CreateSpace with no upfront costs at all.

One area I would definitely not recommend economizing on is editing. I think you should always employ a professional editor, even if you're a much published author – actually, if you're a much published author, I don't need to tell you that.

Editing isn't just a question of tidying up your grammar and punctuation – that's part of it but for me, the least part. A good editor can identify weaknesses or inconsistencies in the structure of your plot; they will tell you if your characters are unconvincing or your settings too sketchy.

If your book is non-fiction, an editor can help identify gaps, inaccuracies and lack of clarity in the information, as well as advising on the use of bullets and boxes, illustrations and diagrams, headings and sub-headings – all the special features of non-fiction that can make it complicated to organise and lay out.

An editor will also tidy up your writing, helping you sort out inelegant phrasing, saggy dialogue, unnecessary detail and other micro-editing issues we can easily miss by simply being too close to the work to see them.

You will want to consider buying your own ISBNs for each version of your book from Nielsen BookScan, so that it can be listed to the book trade under your name, or the name you choose for your publishing company. You can choose any name to publish under, including your own author name; there's no need to incorporate your publisher name until you pass a high earning threshold.

You will also need to register with the IRS if you'll be selling in the US, but this is far easier for non-US nationals than it used to be. I followed the clear instructions on Catherine Ryan Howard's blog.

For my first self-publishing venture, which was a new edition of an out-of-print book for parents and carers, *Help Your Child to Handle Bullying*, I wanted the lowest possible financial outlay and investment of time.

I had no illusions about the sales potential of the subject after half a dozen UK and foreign editions with major publishers had only managed to sell a few thousand copies, but great press reviews and a steady trickle of grateful emails from readers made me feel the book should still be available for parents struggling to help a bullied child.

Because the book had already been published before, and not long enough ago to need any significant updating, I knew the text didn't need editing.

I tried to design a cover using kdp's cover creator but wasn't happy with it so I commissioned a designer on www. fiverr.com, who did a perfectly adequate job for five dollars.

I decided to hand the formatting and distribution over to an aggregator, Draft2Digital. The deal with that kind of service is that they prepare your manuscript for publication, publish it on all the main platforms, such as Apple and Barnes & Noble, and handle all the sales.

Aggregators such as Draft2Digital and Smashwords don't make any upfront charge, but rather retain a royalty of 10-15% of your profit from sales and pay the rest to you every month. So my total outlay for my first self-published book was five dollars and my total effort almost nothing.

But every book is different, and I made different decisions when it came to my second self-published book, *Writing in the House of Dreams*. This was something I'd worked on for years, something I really loved and believed in. I wanted to do the very best I could for it, and I was prepared to invest some of my savings and make a real effort when it came to publicity.

The book had never been published, so my first decision was to hire an editor. This was the most expensive part, and I didn't expect her to find much that needed changing or correcting because I don't usually need a lot of editing when I'm working for traditional publishers.

However, the adjustments my editor was able to suggest definitely made the book feel more clear and consistent, and she helped enormously with suggestions for the layouts.

I wanted my beautiful book to have a beautiful cover, so I hired a designer. She gave me a list of illustration sites to look at and I chose an image from www.istockphoto.com, which cost me eight dollars. The designer created some samples around it, but I didn't like them, and seeing how it looked on a book cover, I wasn't confident that the image I'd chosen would ever really work.

So I started thinking about individual artists whose work I liked, and found a linocut I thought might be suitable on Hilke MacIntyre's website. We agreed a fee and, as I was already working on *When a Writer Isn't Writing*, and wanted to create a brand feel with *Writing in the House of Dreams*, I also paid for permission to use a second image to use on this cover.

Choosing covers was the most stressful part of the process for me because I was very aware that I knew nothing about design and didn't trust my own judgement. I also didn't like going back to the designer to ask for changes, not knowing how much work that would involve.

But on the upside, I enjoyed having control over what my cover would eventually look like. Almost all the covers I've had done by traditional publishers have been on the scale of fine to fabulous, but one or two have been somewhere between disappointing and dire, and it's hard to love and publicise a book you feel looks ugly or naff.

I didn't want to have to learn about formatting; I actually felt that *Writing in the House of Dreams* would be too difficult for me, as it was a complex text which would require several fonts and sizes, boxes for the writing exercises and various complicated extras such as poems and illustrations. So I hired a designer for that job as well.

This way of publishing meant I had to bear more upfront costs, but once it was published I could keep all the profits. If you decide this is the best approach for your book but can't afford the outlay, you could try looking for backers on a crowd-funding site such as www.kickstarter.com

I would certainly consider going with an aggregator again for lower up-front costs, or employing a small team to work on the editing, cover and design; I'd also like, at some stage, to try and do all the formatting and cover design myself for a straightforward work of fiction. What I don't think I personally would consider is paying a company to provide the whole package.

These companies usually charge a big upfront fee plus a healthy percentage of your profit. In exchange, they will create a cover for you, edit, format and distribute your book and provide an ISBN.

You should do your research really well if you feel this is the route for you, and bear in mind that these are businesses and their main purpose is to make money, not to support writers.

Many authors who have gone with self-publishing companies say that the editing and production quality has been substandard, the promised promotions never happened and royalties were not paid on time. What's more, once enrolled, they have faced relentless pressure to spend more and more on new publishing deals and enhanced services.

I would add, don't assume that self-publishing companies linked to major publishers will give you a better chance of securing a mainstream contract. They won't.

The absolute best way to research self-publishing services is by joining online communities of self-published authors, where people exchange their own experiences. The companies themselves tend to make it difficult for you to get a proper overview by using such practices as operating under multiple different names, which appear to be independent when they aren't.

Agents are also feeling their way into helping their authors to self-publish, and this is a good idea in principal. Most authors would happily pay their agent's fees on self-published books, especially if they have been involved in helping to get the manuscript up to a publishable standard, have tried to place it with traditional publishers and will be proactive in seeking foreign deals and looking after the rights.

But you are effectively still on your own with promoting the book, distribution and sales and, at the time of writing this, the kind of self-publishing deal agents are offering doesn't feel very attractive to authors.

As well as losing direct control, the author is expected to pay all the upfront costs and will therefore not be earning until the outlay is recouped, while the agency bears none of the costs but takes their percentage from the very first book sold, because of the time it takes to manage the publication.

Having said that, like the whole publishing world, everything is changing fast, and these author-agent contracts are very much a work-in-progress. I'd certainly say that if you have an agent you should discuss your self-publishing projects and explore the options as to whether and how they can be involved.

Once you have decided which self-publishing route to go down, based on how much time and money you want to invest, the next thing to think about is how much publicity you want to do.

My approach to non-fiction self-publishing was firstly to plan a book about something I am knowledgeable and passionate about – writing for wellbeing. By shaping my book idea to incorporate contributions from local people, I was able to apply for a local arts grant to pay for the printing.

Securing this funding, coupled with tying the subject of the book in with a big project I did at work, meant I could persuade the organisation to let me publish the book in its name, and so get some help with the initial promotion and distribution.

The downside of this is that, while the book cost me nothing but time, there was also no money in it for me (or anyone). I was happy to accept that for my first book in order to get known as an author, for example, the funding allowed me to supply a free copy of the book to every public and education library in the county.

Having worked in journal publishing, I already had the publishing skills I needed to get the book to a print-ready PDF. This reduced the costs of printing, but substantially increased the time I spent publishing the book – 500 hours for 220 pages, A5 format.

The skills I didn't have were in marketing – the biggest challenge for self-publishers – my advice is find out how to do it and get started well before you publish.

Carol Ross

Marketing – the biggest challenge for self-publishers

Most established authors know a lot about publicising their books because they are used to giving talks and interviews, organising their own signings and launches, and reaching readers through their blogs and networks.

They are familiar with publishing schedules and the need to start laying the groundwork well in advance of publication day. They know about sending out review copies and writing press releases.

Fortunately, if you haven't had much publishing experience, none of this is hard to learn and there's plenty of information and advice freely available on the web. You might decide, as I did when I self-published *Help Your Child to Handle Bullying*, that you just want to put the book out there and chasing sales is not enough of a priority for you to take time out from your current writing to do publicity.

But for most new books, I think there's not much point in publishing if you don't try to find readers; it's definitely worth setting aside a couple of months to publicise something that may have taken years to write.

Set a launch date, because that creates a focus you can work up to and plan a campaign around. Ideally your launch date should be at least six months ahead. Write a list of people you could send review copies to, not just the press but book-bloggers too.

Write a list of papers, magazines and local media you could send a press release to, offering an article or interview. Remember there are different run-up times for different media; some magazines will commission articles up to six months ahead, whereas local radio might have a slot to interview you within a couple of days.

Approach local bookshops to see whether they would be willing to host a signing event, and contact your library service to enquire about giving some talks.

If you haven't got a blog, start one. Interact with other

bloggers, especially those who might do an interview with you about your new book, publish a guest post or carry a review.

If you aren't on any social media networks, you're missing some great opportunities, but they won't work instantly for you. You need to build your networks, and you shouldn't leave it until your book is about to come out.

Those are the basics, but there are lots of other things you can do, and although it's all down to you with self-publishing, remember that even if you were traditionally published, your publisher would expect you to be doing a lot of self-promotion too.

Most publicity work is completely unpaid, or even costs you money, so it can actually feel easier to motivate yourself with a self-published book, where you're doing all the publicity but also earning all the profit from your endeavours.

Self-publishers rarely achieve high volume sales, but they don't need to. With royalty rates at 70%, a few hundred sales can net as much money for the author as a few thousand books sold through traditional publishers.

Self-published books can also stay in print and available for as long as you want them to, so they can be a permanent source of income, however small.

The majority of authors make their living from a variety of small sources of income, and the best way forward for those who want to create a sustainable career in writing may be to use both traditional and self-publishing.

The happy hybrid

If you are able to place everything you write with traditional publishers, self-publishing might seem like a time-consuming distraction from what you do best – writing.

> Being published by traditional houses means that you have access to excellent editors and copy-editors, a marketing department, production department, fulfilment house and a publicity person. I would rather spend my working life writing than performing all those functions. It is a better use of my time to write. It is what I am for.
>
> Michelle Lovric

But most authors are not in that enviable position, and you can spend several years working on a book which your agent and the publishers she sends it to feel is of publishable quality, yet it still fails to secure a contract.

That's several years of wasted time, which could be redeemed by a couple of weeks or months bringing it to readers yourself. Self-publishing may mean you have less time for new writing, but it does not mean you are spending less time writing work that will be published.

Self-publishing your unplaced manuscripts doesn't only mean you can earn money from your writing irrespective of the whims of the market; it also protects you psychologically from sinking into despair.

Here is some of the publishers' feedback on my Young Adult novel, *Drift*, which we couldn't get a contract for: 'this is a very fine novel, so subtle, yet sharply observed';

'a sensitive subject, delicately and carefully handled'; 'compelling'; 'highly readable'; 'the writing is very strong'.

I worked on that book, on and off, for more than ten years, so you can imagine how frustrating it felt to get such positive feedback but no publishing deal. Not so long ago, that would have been the end of the road for *Drift*, but now the self-publishing option means all that time, work and passion need not go completely to waste.

The same thing goes for books that have gone out of print, which can happen these days very quickly. You've still taken months or years to write them, and all you've got to show for it is a pitifully low advance. Being able to bring them back to the market yourself is very healing.

Traditionally published authors can supplement their income by self-publishing their unpublished manuscripts and out of print books, that's a no-brainer, but they can also earn more, in certain circumstances, by going straight to self-publishing. It makes sense now to decide which way to publish on a book-by-book basis.

Specialist non-fiction is a case in point. If you are an expert in your field, you may be in a position where anything you write could have a guaranteed but limited sales potential. Most of your prospective buyers will be within your networks, and you don't need a publisher because you have direct access to your readers yourself.

I decided to go straight to self-publishing with this book because I teach writing workshops and blog about writing, so I'm in constant contact with people who might be interested in buying a copy. I have a track record in writing about writing, with my traditionally published children's book *How To Be a Brilliant Writer*.

Another reason I chose self-publishing is because I wanted to get a second adults' book about writing out as soon as possible, to help sales of my newly published *Writing in the House of Dreams*.

Traditional publishing is a very slow process; it can take several weeks for your agent to read your manuscript, then up to a year waiting for publishers to read it and make a decision. After the manuscript has been accepted, it normally takes eighteen months to publish a book, and the eBook is often held back to protect bookshop sales of the paperback.

With self-publishing, you can bring a book to market almost instantly, which means you can build a body of work quickly. You are also earning as soon as the writing is finished, rather than wasting time trying to get a publishing deal which may never materialize and then, if it does, waiting another eighteen months to see it in print.

The speed of self-publishing makes it a particularly good option for books that are really topical and need to catch the moment. Kate Harrison wrote and self-published her book on the 5:2 diet the minute it hit the headlines after a documentary on TV.

I've self-published two non-fiction books on Kindle, with help from my agent (*The 5:2 Diet Book* and *5:2 Your Life*). The huge benefits are speed – and the fact you can change them and update them easily – plus having control of marketing, price and promotions. It taught me so much that is also very helpful with my traditionally published books. In fact, both books then got 'traditional' deals, which are still worth having because a publisher can produce a far more attractive 'real' book at a better price for consumers, and have much better distribution.

Kate Harrison

Kate caught the moment with a new book. Another friend, Jennie Walters, saw the same opportunity with her out-of-print series, 'Swallowcliffe Hall', when 'Downton Abbey' became a global phenomenon.

Thank you, Amazon, and thank you, Kindle. I'm facing the future with more confidence as a writer than I've had for ages – and all because I've released my *'Swallowcliffe Hall'* historical trilogy as eBooks. It's been fantastic, a positive experience from the start. Sales might start falling off tomorrow but right now, it feels like my books have been given a new lease of life.

So here's the story. The series was published in print about six years ago. An editor signed me up on the strength of three synopses and a few chapters and everyone seemed filled with enthusiasm. I began researching Victorian country houses in earnest, found wonderful quotes from contemporary servants' manuals and etiquette guides to open each chapter, and enjoyed writing my first historical fiction.

Unfortunately my lovely editor rushed to commission the covers before she went off on maternity leave, and we ended up with two girls staring glumly out of a sepia background; the third cover was a bit jollier but it didn't match the others. With my editor away, there was no one to champion my series and, by the time I was writing the third book, it was obvious these were not going to be bestsellers. There were hardly any foreign rights deals, reviews or promotions from the bookshop chains. Even my bookmarks had typos. I felt a failure. I couldn't tell anyone I was a writer; I didn't have the right.

When 'Downton Abbey' was such a success a few years later, I suggested issuing the stories as a three-in-one collection with a more enticing cover, to tie in with the second TV series, but the proposal was vetoed. I knew, though, that I would spontaneously combust with envy and frustration if I had to watch another series of Downton without doing something for my poor languishing stories.

So my agent got the rights back (because hardly any copies had been sold over the last few royalty periods) and suggested I turn them into eBooks. My first formatting steps were tentative but, encouraged by guidance and enthusiasm from fellow authors and by a stroke of luck in having a talented designer friend, I persevered.

I photographed a lovely old house in Dorset, trawled through family photographs and spent hours picture-researching on the Internet before sending the material to my friend. Hooray! I love the covers she designed! Shamelessly, I gave the books 'Downton Abbey' tags wherever I could – the prospect of reaching an audience hungry for British nostalgia being too tempting to ignore – and waited to see what would happen.

People began to buy them. Not in huge quantities

at first, and I'm still not going to rival Amanda Hocking, but now I'm selling steadily in America as well as the UK, and to adults as well as teens.

Epublishing has shown me a way past the gatekeepers (bookshops with limited space, overseas publishers with full lists), straight to my readers. And the wonderful thing is, there's no longer a two-week window in which the books' fate will be decided by bookshops returning unsold copies and refusing to stock any more; my book can be available for as long as I choose, to anyone, anywhere, who looks for it or comes across it.

Now I don't have to feel apologetic any more. I've been empowered, liberated. So thank you, Amazon, and here's to an exciting new future for writers and readers everywhere!

Jennie Walters

The publishing scene has changed beyond recognition in the twenty years since I was first published. Back then, the goal was to find an agent and a publisher who loved your writing, and would view you as a long-term commitment.

Nobody expected you to have a bestseller with your first book. You built your readership gradually; you matured as a writer within these two stable relationships, and you earned a modest but liveable income from advances and royalties.

In a hard-hitting interview with the Bookseller in 2014, the Society of Authors' Chief Executive, Nicola Solomon, said most authors would still prefer to be traditionally published but the terms publishers were demanding were 'no longer fair or sustainable'.

For a few years, before the advent of self-publishing, being an author was starting to feel pretty bleak. Growing financial pressures made it hard to see how you could survive in the business; growing creative pressures made you wonder whether you wanted to.

Authors had no option but to accept whatever deal was offered, because there was no other viable way to bring their book to market. The opportunity to publish your own work and to publicise it too, via social media, has gone some way to restoring the balance of power.

Authors don't have to go desperately cap-in-hand, grateful for any crumbs that fall from the publishers' tables, because now they have a choice. The fact that they can earn a 70% royalty on self-published eBooks gives power to their argument with the publishers over the 'industry standard rate' of 25%, and successful self-publishers can set their own terms.

For example, Catherine Quinn says her instructions to her agent are that she will only consider offers from publishers above the level she could earn if she self-published the work as an eBook, going on her current track record.

Hugh Howie, author of the phenomenally successful *Wool*, which he chose to self-publish in the first instance, only sold the print rights to Simon and Schuster; he did not agree to give them film and eBook rights.

The self-publishing option has also restored the creative joy and freedom of being a writer, because we can write what we want to write, knowing it can be published, and not have to try and tailor everything to an increasingly bestseller-driven market.

An added bonus for women is that self-publishing has leveled the playing field. In traditional publishing, male writers have always earned more and been more highly valued and recognized, with 80% of the Telegraph's '100 novels everyone should read', 70% of their 'Best books of 2014' and 85% of the Guardian's '100 greatest novels of all time' all being written by men.

Far more women write, read and buy books, and when you take out the establishment and let readers decide what they like best, as happens with self-publishing, nearly 70% of sales are currently books written by women.

Orna Ross, who set up the Alliance of Independent Authors, thinks every author should try it at least once. My first experience of self-publishing a previously unpublished title was tough, but I'm so glad I persevered.

Although on the one hand I felt frequently out of my depth, having to research and learn how the production and business side of things worked, on the other hand I experienced all that as an exhilarating extension of the creative process.

I felt like William Blake, inventing his own printing method to produce his own books, beavering away on his own, with no expectation of financial success. It reminded me of the way I felt as a little girl, creating my own books out of pages sewn together between cardboard covers made from cereal boxes.

In many ways, self-publishing suits my temperament and my values, and I know I will want it to be part of my writing life from now on, as well as traditional publishing.

Summing Up

When you are pondering publication:

- make sure your book is of publishable quality
- understand the economics and don't give up the day job
- accept you will have to do most of your own publicity and start building your networks
- try to get a traditional deal to establish your credentials
- look upon self-publishing as a viable alternative.

If you want to make a career in writing, become a happy hybrid.

8 When You Find Your Flow

'I would write a book if I had the time.'

I get this response fairly often when I tell people what I do for a living. I used to find it mildly insulting, but these days I just think it's odd.

Would they say 'I'd do a gall-bladder operation if I had the time' if they met a surgeon? Would they tell their hairdresser they'd do a cut and blow dry, or their accountant they'd put together a financial package, if only they had the time?

Occasionally, someone will come to workshops, never having done any writing whatsoever, because they've decided to write a novel so they can give up the day job. They tend to lose interest when they realise that writing is the same as any other skill; if you want to do it well enough to earn your living from it, that's going to take hard work, learning and practice.

But most people come to writing out of curiosity, for the adventure, and are delighted to find that they love it, and want to do more.

I was taken by surprise by the writing bug, and came late to it. It's been a major part of my life ever since, and I can't imagine ever being without it. It's sustained me through good times and bad, through births and deaths, it's made me happy and miserable, and my one regret is that I didn't start when I was younger. When people say, 'I'm going to write a book one day,' I want to scream at them, 'Do it! Do it now! Stop talking about it – just write!'

Valerie Wilding

Discovering the joy of writing doesn't only give you the impetus to start and keep going, and so build your stamina and skills through practice; it also motivates you to overcome your blocks.

Because whatever your goals and ambitions, even if you have no desire to be published or try and earn your living from writing, you are bound to face setbacks and challenges.

Your blocks are your teachers

Blocks are part of the learning process, whatever you are trying to learn. They are where you come up against the limits of your current understanding and need to take a mental leap.

Every writer is different, and therefore every writer comes up against different blocks. For example, you might have no difficulty getting started, but tend to always run out of steam a few chapters in, whereas someone else might be unable to get past the blank first page.

And what stops you from keeping going might not be the same as what stops another writer with the same problem. For you, it might be cold feet because fear of failure sets in; for them, it might be not knowing how to hold their focus as the plot becomes more complicated.

There is information in your personal blocks. They show you what you personally need to learn. Sometimes it will be a purely technical problem, such as not understanding how subplots work, or what to do about a saggy middle.

When you can't go on because you haven't the skills, your block makes you stop and do some research. You might read some books on the craft of writing, sign up for some courses or find an experienced writer who is willing to mentor you.

The cause of your block may be harder to pin down if it isn't an obvious skills deficit but rather a psychological challenge that you need to address. Writing requires certain character strengths that you may already possess in spades, but some that you might need to work on.

Here are some of the requirements of writing.

Courage

There can be all sorts of fear-based blocks, including fear of failure or success, of criticism or exposure, fear of standing up and being counted, fear of giving offence.

Different people are afraid of different things. If fear stops you from writing, you need to find out what the fear is and face up to it. Your fear-based block will teach you to be more brave.

Patience

In our culture, we think effort and activity equals productivity but, in writing, sometimes months of apparent inactivity, of pondering and daydreaming, can be the laying down of roots from which a whole book will eventually spring quickly and easily.

Creativity is a natural process, a breathing in and breathing out, a rhythm of receptive and productive time, of surrender and control.

Every book requires inspiration as well as perspiration, the same as every creative work. The same as every life. Every block, of whatever kind, teaches you to be more patient, to take the long view, value stillness and respect your writing nature.

Playfulness

Someone once remarked at her first workshop that she hadn't expected it to feel so playful. She had expected instruction, the red pen and homework, but it felt more like messing around in the sandpit at playschool.

I was happy with that because many adults find adopting a childlike attitude of openness and experimentation hard to achieve, but it is absolutely essential in the early stages of writing. Creativity is not a function of the rational mind, as CG Jung observed, but of the play instinct. He said the creative mind 'plays with the objects it loves'.

If the rational mind refuses to let go, it puts on the stern judge's robes of the inner critic, and condemns you to a writing life of struggles and false starts.

A block that feels as if you've been banging your head against a brick wall means it's time to stop, rest your sore head and open your mind; this kind of block wants you to play around with different ways forward, or allow yourself to get distracted and let fresh ideas and clarity come in.

Independence

Writing requires you to be alone for long periods of time, not only alone at your computer but, during the receptive times, alone with your thoughts. This might not be a problem for you, but other people might consider it weird and antisocial, especially in a modern world where sociability is considered a measure of sanity.

Other people might also want to measure your success according to your public profile and income, and not understand why you would want to keep writing if you aren't earning good money from it.

As most writers could earn a better hourly rate doing office work, choosing to write means choosing different values.

If you sometimes stop because you wonder what the point is in doing something that takes you away from your social life and doesn't earn you any money, and yet you really don't want to stop, your block will teach you to walk your own path, guided by creative values, measuring your success not by your bank statements but by your creative achievements and personal satisfaction.

Self-acceptance

Writing will show you things about yourself that you might not have realised or noticed. Maeve Binchy, in *The Maeve Binchy Writers' Club*, says she made the uncomfortable discovery that she was a moraliser.

One of the things I've discovered about myself, through writing, is that I'm horribly worthy; I want to help. It's an unwelcome discovery because I would far rather be the kind of writer who simply wants to entertain.

Your writing might show you that you're much more grumpy than you thought, or more sentimental, or more grandiose.

If you don't like what you discover but you still want to write, you'll need to get over it, because you are what you are, and it will inevitably show in your writing. I hit a hiccup for a while, trying to unhitch my wagon from wanting to help, but things have gone smoothly again since I threw up my hands and said 'What the heck? I am who I am' and reframed it as wanting to share the good stuff.

Trust

With writing, you need to be able to tolerate a high degree of uncertainty. You might spend a whole year working on a novel only to find, once it's done, that it doesn't hold together.

Or maybe it will be everything you hoped it would be and publishers will love it, but it still won't get a contract, or it will get a contract but go out of print almost straight away. Maybe it will bring you fame and fortune, but maybe it will bring you nothing except bad reviews.

Writing is a long, hard labour of love, with absolutely no way of knowing what the outcome will be. The only way you can keep going is if you learn to travel hopefully, and trust that whatever happens, you will handle it.

Dedication

Anyone who teaches writing workshops will know that the people with the most natural ability are not necessarily the ones who achieve the greatest writing success.

The ones who do best at not only selling their work but also honing and developing their skills are the ones who love writing, value their natural ability and have the dedication to keep working at it.

Becoming a writer is not easy but, like anything that's hard won, as you accept the challenges and make the changes writing asks of you, you will reap rewards and be able to take pride in your achievements.

Because it was what I always wanted, and because I fought very long and very hard for it, achieving publication has given me some confidence and some pride, though I do have to keep reminding myself to feel proud, as it's still very easy to feel crushed. But it hasn't made me satisfied. And it hasn't made the writing any easier at all – possibly the opposite!

Nicola Morgan

Writing will go on challenging you because its possibilities are boundless, but the more you do it, the easier it is to keep going, because you're learning from experience how to tackle your blocks and as the challenges diminish you notice the benefits even more.

Writing is a way of being

Published or unpublished, public or private, writing brings about a personal transformation for the writer. Non-writers think only in terms of the products of writing, such as books, poems and journals, but writers know there's much more to it than that.

Writing isn't just about words on the page – it's a different way of being. It changes your experience of the world, and deepens your experience of your self.

Writing changes your experience of the world

Most people go through life like a dreamer within a dream, unaware of its structures and qualities, but writers are like lucid dreamers; they become an observer as well as a participant.

One very successful Young Adult author told me she often catches herself narrating her life as she lives it. 'She's going to the front door, but she really doesn't want to, because she knows who it will be...'

Writers tend to transform events into fictional shapes, and that makes them more aware of the way that everyone makes sense of experience by shaping it into coherent narratives, so every life is a fiction, and every person it's author, although they aren't usually aware of the story-making mind at work.

Writing also helps us notice how extraordinary our ordinary lives really are. We tend not to value the familiar; we take it for granted, and don't find it particularly interesting.

But when you look at the familiar things of your life through a writer's eyes, you see them from outside, from how a reader might see them. Your day-to-day in a farmhouse in the middle of the moor will seem exotic and strange to anyone who lives in a city; your Soho lifestyle will be interesting and different to people who live in a village.

Writers plunder their own lives all the time for settings and themes, and writing about them means re-experiencing them from a different perspective.

As well as heightening your awareness of the stories and settings of your life, being a writer intensifies the way you experience the world through your senses. You notice the sounds, sights, smells that you might use if you were writing about the place you're in; you notice the effects of emotions in your physical body.

Because you are always immersing yourself in another person, facing their problems and feeling their feelings, you develop greater empathy for others. This is one way in which writing, at the same time as teaching you to love being alone, creates a strong connection with other people.

It connects you with your characters in the most intimate way possible; it also connects you with your readers, allowing you to occupy their head-space with your own thoughts and ideas. It connects you with your tribe of other writers, and with the whole culture in which you are developing ideas and creating art.

Writing makes life bigger by giving you somewhere else to go, a sanctuary in times of trouble, a place of solace in times of grief. Boundless worlds of imagination when the real world feels too narrow and constrained.

When you are a writer, there are no times of boredom. Ordinary life may be what it may be, but the life of the imagination is always interesting and exciting, and available 24:7.

Just as writing makes your life feel bigger and more resonant, it also expands and deepens your experience of yourself.

Writing deepens your experience of yourself

Young children are magical thinkers; for them, everything is possible, from talking animals to wicked witches and ogres. The magical world can be a scary place, but fortunately parents, grandparents and carers have magical powers to keep the child safe.

Magical thinking works when your whole world is your home, but as children start to engage with the world outside, where they have no protectors, they must learn to think in a different way. They have to develop a more focused, logical, organising mind.

Adults are rational thinkers but, when you write, you have to re-inhabit the magical mind of the child you once were, which is still inside you, but overlaid and fallen from view. You learn to relax your rational mind and allow the magic to re-emerge, by putting yourself into the 'writer's trance'.

But it isn't the same as being a child, because when you come back to the magic as an adult, you are able to observe and discover the nature of the magical mind, without being overwhelmed.

You discover there is an abundant flow of images and

stories running through the deeper levels of your consciousness all the time, like dreams. It has no beginning and no end; it is all movement, never stopping, producing new images and stories as soon as the old ones die away.

You may also notice that, like dreams, the products of your imagination are mysteriously connected to your real life, with your deep mind constantly engaged in creating story versions of your conscious thoughts, emotions and experiences.

You glimpse the depth and texture of your self, and find that, just as a story you are writing is the visible tip of the iceberg of your knowledge about it, so your rational mind is the visible tip of the iceberg of your psyche.

Moving up and down through these deeper layers of the self puts ordinary life in a larger context. It gives you a sense of proportion, and makes life feel much more stable than when you were living entirely on the surface.

How does being a writer change the way I live? I guess it kind of keeps me sane, keeps me level. When I'm not writing, my life can quite easily begin to feel a bit unstructured. Little things get to me more; things feel less under control. When I'm writing, it helps straighten out my feelings about life in general, and everything just seems to work more smoothly.

Liz Kessler

When I'm not writing, I feel scattered. I feel like I'm trying to hold onto everything, but not managing to get a good grasp on anything at all. I long to let go.

Writing means letting go of the limited world of reality

and surrendering yourself into the boundless world of imagination. In happiness science, when you lose yourself in an activity, that is called 'flow'.

When you find your writing flow, sometimes it will be fast and sometimes slow. This book has taken six months to write; *Writing in The House of Dreams* took well over ten years.

Sometimes the flow will be deep, and sometimes shallow. Sometimes you may feel completely becalmed although later, when you are able to take the long view, you will see that something was always happening, something was being achieved.

When you are in the flow of writing, blocks can no more stop it than boulders can stop a stream. They are part of its character; they make it what it is.

Blocks are not a problem in the process of writing, but an essential part of it, showing where you need to pause and take stock, gather information, develop new skills, correct an attitude or challenge a fear.

Changing the way you look at your blocks is the key to finding your flow.

Summing Up

Everyone is different and therefore every writer will face different challenges in their writing; your blocks show you what you personally need to learn.

If you are willing to go the hard yards, writing will change the way you experience life, and give you access to deeper levels of your self.

When you find your writing flow you know that words on the page are just a stage; a writer is always writing.

Websites and Organisations Mentioned in this Book

These are just services and resources that I happen to have used and can recommend, or that writing friends have recommended to me – it's obviously not a comprehensive list.

The Alliance of Independent Authors
<http://allianceindependentauthors.org>
Fantastic resource for authors who self-publish or are planning to.

The Authors' Licensing and Collecting Society <http://www.alcs.co.uk>
Organisation set up to protect the rights of authors and ensure they receive fair payment for the various uses of their work.

Catherine Ryan Howard
<http://catherineryanhoward.com>
Interesting blog with excellent instructions for self-published authors on how to register for US tax exemption.

Cornerstones <http://cornerstones.co.uk>
UK literary consultancy where you can send your manuscript for a detailed appraisal, which includes its market potential.

CreateSpace <https://www.createspace.com>
Amazon's print-on-demand paperback publishing service, straightforward to use and offering a range of levels of support.

Draft2Digital <https://www.draft2digital.com>
Self-publishing aggregator – they will format, publish and distribute your book for no upfront fee but a 10% share of sales. Very friendly and helpful people, and a site that's easy to use.

Girls Heart Books <http://girlsheartbooks.com>
Team blog written by children's authors for their young readers. A good model for people who want to blog but not often enough to run their own site.

istockphoto <http://www.istockphoto.com>
Great source of images for book covers; you can buy the right to use them for a small fee.

Kickstarter <https://www.kickstarter.com>
Crowdfunding site where people can seek or make investments in creative projects.

Kindle Direct Publishing <https://kdp.amazon.com>
Amazon's ebook publishing service, for selling through amazon stores worldwide.

Lapidus <http://www.lapidus.org.uk>
Organisation that promotes writing as an opportunity for healing and personal development.

Neilson BookScan <http://www.nielsenbookscan.co.uk>
This is where you can buy ISBNs and put your books on the register for wholesalers, retailers and libraries.

Pat Neill <https://astrolifecoach.wordpress.com>
Astrologer and life coach, based in the UK but able to
offer consultations via Skype, FaceTime or phone.

Public Lending Right <https://www.plr.uk.com>
UK and Ireland organisation that administers
payments for library loans to published authors who
sign up and register their books.

Smashwords <https://www.smashwords.com>
The world's largest distributor of indie ebooks.

The Society of Authors <http://www.societyofauthors.org>
Professional body protecting the rights and interests of
authors. Personal advice, contract vetting, social and
training events and specialist groups for members.

Fiverr <https://uk.fiverr.com>
Wide range of creative services such as cover design
and illustration, at very low prices.

Some Brilliant Books on Writing

There are loads of great books on writing - these are just a few that I love. Those nearest the top of the list are the ones I return to most often.

Brande, Dorothea *Becoming a Writer*
A brilliant starting point for thinking about yourself as a writer.

Goldberg, Natalie *Writing Down the Bones : Freeing the Writer Within*
My personal favourite – a kind of tao of writing.

Hughes, Ted *Poetry in the Making: A Handbook for Writing and Teaching*
Absolutely wonderful writing about writing.

Hill, Bekki *Coach Yourself to Writing Success*
Practical advice on how to set your writing goals and work towards them.

King, Stephen *On Writing*
A mix of method and memoir from a master story-teller.

Maass, Donald *Writing the Breakout Novel: Winning Advice from a Top Agent and His Best-selling Client*
A top agent talks about taking your writing to the next level.

Cameron, Julia *The Artist's Way: A Course in Discovering and Recovering Your Creative Self*
Lots of writers love and use this book for busting through blocks.

Lamott, Anne *Bird by Bird: Instructions on Writing and Life*
Thoughtful and thought-provoking on the subject of writing and the writer's life.

Campbell, Joseph *The Hero with a Thousand Faces*
The original exposition of the hero's journey through myths and legends from different cultures.

Vogler, Christopher *The Writer's Journey: Mythic Structure for Writers*
A screenwriter's exploration of the hero's journey as a story structure.

About the Author

Since her first book was published in 1994, Jenny Alexander has written about 150 books for children and adults, a dozen articles in national magazines, several interactive CDRoms and a writing app.

Jenny teaches the art and craft of writing fiction, non-fiction and memoir. She also runs a variety of innovative workshops, which enable writers to draw on creative dream techniques, image work and tarot.

Her book on creative dreaming for writers, described by poet Victoria Field as 'wonderful and unique', is *Writing in the House of Dreams*.

Jenny's workshops taught me to stop panicking about my creativity and to start listening properly to my own inner thoughts. I've used her workshop ideas again and again to help me cope with creative problems.

Moira Butterfield
<http://www.moirabutterfield.com>

In one short session she showed me the possibilities for taking my writing somewhere else, and now I am working on new ideas that expand what I learnt with her.

Alison Boyle
<http://www.oxfordwriters.com/about-us>

During Jenny's collage workshop, which she led with a soulful gentleness, I had a sense that disparate parts of my mind spoke their sorrows and dreams, and discovered they all wanted the same things. Several years on, I am still nourished by the clarity and the freedom that emerged from the sweetness and excitement of that afternoon.

Moira Munro

<http://www.moiramunro.com>

Acknowledgements

I'd like to thank all the authors who have kindly shared their experience and wisdom in this book:

Cas Lester <www.caslester.com>
Avril Joy <www.avriljoy.com>
Kate Harrison <http://kate-harrison.com>
Sean Callery <www.seancallery.co.uk>
Moira Munro <www.moiramunro.com>
Adèle Geras <www.adelegeras.com>
Valerie Wilding <www.valeriewilding.co.uk>
Heather Dyer <www.heatherdyer.co.uk>
Rosalie Warren <www.rosalie-warren.co.uk>
Linda Newbery <www.lindanewbery.co.uk>
Nicola Morgan <https://www.nicolamorgan.com>
Meg Harper <https://megharperbooks.wordpress.com>
Michelle Lovric <www.michellelovric.com>
Miriam Halahmy <www.miriamhalahmy.com>
Patricia Elliott <www.patriciaelliott.co.uk>
Diana Kimpton <www.dianakimpton.co.uk>
Carol Ross <https://trioross.wordpress.com>
Lynne Benton <www.lynnebenton.com>
Jennie Walters <www.jenniewalters.com>
Abi Burlingham <www.abiburlingham.com>
Vangile Makwakwa <http://wealthy-money.com>

Thanks also to my beta readers, Lynne Benton, Abi Burlingham, Sarah Mackie and Gill Payne, for their invaluable feedback and advice, and to everyone who has attended my workshops, and taught me so much.

Final Word

I wrote this book for the same reason I teach workshops, because writing has been a source of joy and revelation to me throughout my life, and I love to share the good stuff.

If you have enjoyed reading it, or found something useful in its pages, I hope you will take a moment to share the good stuff too, by telling your friends and posting a short review on the website where you bought it.

Many thanks indeed!

Jenny Alexander

Writing in the House of Dreams: Unlock the Power of Your Unconscious Mind

Creative ideas spring spontaneously from the unconscious like dreams, but the critical, rational mind can get in the way. Free things up with this unusual guide by seasoned author and writing tutor, Jenny Alexander, which is packed with practical tips and exercises to help you

- enter the dream or 'writer's trance' at will, through intention and surrender
- explore the unique landscapes, themes and images of your personal unconscious
- increase your dream awareness to boost your writing
- use writing to deepen your understanding of dreams
- enter the mythic dimension, where 'big dreams' and bestsellers are born

A fascinating mixture of handbook and autobiography. I learnt things, my mind was opened and it was a damn good read.
                    Nicola Morgan, author and public speaker

Wonderful and unique.
                    Victoria Field, writer and poetry therapist.

Get Writing!

Writing for 20 minutes a day is a tried and tested way of breaking through writer's block, and Jenny Alexander's app, *Get Writing!*, delivers a new writing task to your iPhone or iPad every day for 28 days.

What makes *Get Writing!* unique is that it's structured towards creating a finished piece in that 20 minutes a day. There are 4 stages, each consisting of 7 writing tasks:

Stage 1: Start writing
Stage 2: Fire up your imagination
Stage 3: Write a complete story
Stage 4: Redraft and make it better

So what are you waiting for? Download it from the Apple App Store and get writing!

Lightning Source UK Ltd.
Milton Keynes UK
UKHW01f1933080518
322295UK00001B/158/P